Pulling Together

PRAISE FOR *PULLING TOGETHER*

In this handbook for community change lies the scaffolding for bringing aliveness and economic vitality into every neighborhood and community that we care about. Puts our attention on our own local gifts and capacities, sidesteps the futility of waiting for the transformation of people in charge or elected, and is the realization of democracy within very local hands — Peter Block, author, *Activating the Common Good*

It's easy right now to believe that democracy is finished and to feel that there isn't much a person can do to change that. This book is an antidote to that. It is a treasure trove of stories that are evidence that democracy still works. — Katherine Cramer, author, *The Politics of Resentment*

This practical and accessible book, written by people whose advice is grounded in experience, will give you a step-by-step map of what comes next. It's a treasure-trove of hard-earned wisdom about positive and lasting social change. — Parker J. Palmer, author, *Healing the Heart of Democracy: The Courage to Create a Politics Worthy of the Human Spirit*

Real stories of ordinary people who changed things for the better and an easy-to-understand framework for organizing that can be applied to almost any situation. Teaches you how to work together in a time that seems intent upon tearing us apart. — Ayla Boylen, President, Our Future, Cedar Rapids, Iowa

A field manual for how to change rural communities marked by heartbreaking economic decline yet sustained by the incredible resilience of the people living there. — Brian Reisinger, award-winning author of *Land Rich, Cash Poor: My Family's Hope and the Untold History of the Disappearing American Farmer*

If you're looking for shortcuts — the right "message," the charismatic leader, some social media gimmick — this is not the book for you. If you're looking for ways to create ongoing and sustainable change, it is. — Michael Gecan, author, *Going Public: An Organizer's Guide to Citizens' Action* and *People's Institutions in Decline*

Pulling Together

A Handbook for Community Change

TOM MOSGALLER and
MIKE BREININGER

acta

PULLING TOGETHER
A Handbook for Community Change

by Tom Mosgaller and Mike Breininger

cover art "Working Together" by Eva Pratt
edited by Gregory F. Augustine Pierce
designed and typeset by Andrea Reider
proofread by Timothy Coldwell

Published by ACTA Publications
7135 W. Keeney Street, Niles, IL 60714
www.actapublications.com, 800-397-2282

ISBN: 978-0-87946-742-5

Library of Congress Control Number: 2024948111

Printed in the U.S.A. by Total Printing Systems
Years: 35 32 33 32 31 30 29 28 27 26 25
Printing 10 9 8 7 6 5 4 3 2 First

Text printed on 30% post-consumer recycled paper

DEDICATION

To all the people who pull together
to use the power of their hands, hearts, and heads
to leave their communities
better than they found them.

CONTENTS

FOREWORD

by John McKnight and Jeff Yost

There is a reason the authors called this a "handbook." They want to get it in the hands of those who might need a nudge or a simple set of tools to make their communities better—things they may have forgotten or were never taught in high school civics class about making change that matters. They have worked to cut out the jargon and fancy language that sometimes stops ordinary people from taking on new opportunities or things that need fixing in their communities.

❦

The two of us have both spent most of our lives doing, encouraging, teaching, and writing about the power of people working together in communities big and small, urban and rural.

Over the years, we each have seen what bottom-up, relationally based, citizen-led community building looks like. We've experienced the power of the stories that have been passed on by citizen to citizen, neighbor to neighbor, and town to town. Stories are to communities what grease is to a squeaky wheel: a lubricant. Stories free up the various parts of society, get them moving, and tap into the good will and imaginations of those who care enough to act together with their neighbors to accomplish something. When people hear stories like those in this book, they believe that if someone else, "someone just like me," can do it, so can they!

We know Tom Mosgaller, Mike Breininger, and the other storytellers who contributed to this handbook have done the work and learned the lessons. Now we can all benefit from learning what they've learned as champions of positive community change.

$$\sim$$

From the first time we read the manuscript and agreed to do this foreword, we knew this handbook was different. First, it aims to empower ordinary people. Second, it starts with the stories and only then backs into the lessons that are rolled up in what the authors call a "Change Framework." And third, the book provides the tools you, the reader, need to assess your own unique situation and improve your odds of achieving your own dreams for your community.

This handbook is an antidote to the politics of polarization. The stories and the use of the Change Framework can give you a way to build relationships on things that bridge rather than divide, create trust rather than tribes, and get some good work done. Whether it's cleaning up the creek, saving the soil, getting young people to move back to small rural hometowns, providing early childhood development to every family, or helping marginalized people achieve the dream of becoming first-time homeowners—this handbook provides small steps that get the wheels turning.

The compilers and contributors don't duck the issues of power and politics. They know all too well that if you are going to disrupt the status quo it will take power. And no matter what actions you take, they will be political. The difference is that your actions will be the actions of ordinary people using their innate power to engage their neighbors in achieving their collective dreams, not giving away their power to someone else to do it for them. If done well, the kinds of efforts described in this handbook will build nonpartisan community power where the residents are the co-producer of their own future.

❦

Do you remember the first time you had that overpowering urge to ride a bike?

No amount of resistance—fear, anxiety, or butterflies in the pit of your stomach were going to stop you! Do you recall the powerful feeling you had when you sat on the seat, grabbed the handlebars, and pushed off successfully for the first time? The butterflies be damned, you were going to learn to ride so you could explore your neighborhood. If you were like the two of us, you probably wobbled a bit, but undaunted you progressed, you got better, and soon that steady hand that held the seat (mom, dad, a friend) was able to let go. The experience became a lesson in doing something by yourself and for yourself (albeit with a bit of help); and, as they say, the rest is history or, better yet, an inspiring story to tell others.

The authors and contributors built this handbook around three powerful questions:

1. What can we do ourselves?
2. What can we do with a little help from our own neighbors and networks?
3. What other allies do we need to succeed?

Here are simple principles and practices that will improve the odds of your success. All three questions are important, but the work always begins with "what can we do ourselves: right here, right now, right where we are, with what we've already got?"

As you dive into this handbook, the common theme behind the three questions, the many stories, and the Change Framework is that community improvement happens along the lines of relationships only at the speed of trust. If stories are the grease to lubricate your community imagination, then relationships are the glue that bonds it all together. Trusting relationships provide the power you need to catalyze and sustain the positive change you seek.

ᴄ∿⟩

We encourage you to use this handbook to start sketching out your own plans of action. As you read the stories, you will see how the storytellers began by building relationships, taking small actions, and patiently and persistently building the collective power they needed to get results.

On second thought, maybe community building isn't quite as easy as taking that first bike ride. But with the steady hand and encouragement of these veteran community builders, you can be the changemaker you have been preparing all your life to become.

ᴄ∿⟩

John McKnight is co-founder of the Asset Based Community Development (ABCD) Institute. He is recognized globally as a community development visionary, sage, and storyteller. John co-authored with John Kretzmann the original basic ABCD guide, *Building Communities from the Inside Out,* and authored its current version, *The Connected Community.*

Jeff Yost is President and CEO of the Nebraska Community Foundation (NCF). For the past twenty-five years, NCF has inspired leaders and residents in over 250 Nebraska communities to take charge, inspire change, and stimulate their local economies.

INTRODUCTION

࿐

THE CHANGE FRAMEWORK

BY TOM MOSGALLER AND MIKE BREININGER

Community building is a dynamic and living process.
Imagine your community as a giant puzzle, waiting to be improved. Enter the Change Framework, our formula designed to bring about positive transformations. Think of it as a recipe blending three essential elements: Desire (D), Vision (V), and Power (P). These are the key ingredients that can help your community flourish.

Here's a breakdown of how the Change Framework succeeds. Let's start with a real story of two real people trying to make real change in a real community. It is our story.

Our collaboration could easily have been a story of division and opposition, but instead it illustrates how the habits of the heart trump the habits of the head. We two don't see eye to eye on a lot of things, but when it comes to lifting up people, building community, and making a difference where we live, we are both like-hearted and like-minded.

Mike is a small town conservative, evangelical pastor, a leader in his community, and a man who raised a family of sixteen kids—seven biological and nine adopted. Tom on the other hand is progressive, an Episcopalian, a farmer, and a military veteran shaped by years of successful community organizing in both urban and rural areas.

In a world often defined by stark contrasts and ideological divisions, what transpired between us is a remarkable collaboration spanning over a decade, fueled by a shared vision between us: to leave our varied communities better than we found them. Our story, and those of the other storytellers in this handbook, is a testimony to the power of tolerance over tribalism; an unwavering anchoring in shared values, not divisions; and a belief that people can forge bonds of love and trust powerful enough to withstand the tides of polarization.

It is only when you hear our common origin story that you can see what binds us together in spite of our differences.

ᒓᔥᕀ

Tom grew up on a small northern Wisconsin dairy farm that has been in the family since the 1880s. His dad, Frank, and his mom, Mary, like their parents and grandparents before them, were farmers. Like many small farmers with dreams of a better life, Frank farmed by day and was a Class A welder by night, building Great Lakes freighters. Eighteen-hour days were the norm, hard work was a given.

At the age of four, Tom joined the labor force, assisting his mother in the strawberry patches, cherry and apple orchards, and milking barn to make the money the family needed for "incidentals"—shoes, clothes, and school supplies. There were no extravagant birthday parties, no summer vacations, yet a steadfast belief endured in the Mosgaller family that diligence, neighborly goodwill, and adherence to principles would pave the way to progress. The American Dream was alive and well for them.

And then there's Mike, the son of Jerry, a city boy from New York, who once served as a water boy for the construction workers building the Empire State Building. Following his service in the South Pacific during World War II, Jerry returned to New York City, where thousands were recreating the Manhattan skyline. Yet, in the depths of his heart, he harbored a distinct aspiration—a yearning for the pastoral life of a farmer.

In a bold move, Mike's parents embarked on an audacious journey. They uprooted their family and set out for Wisconsin, his mother Marion's home state. There the Breininger family confronted the steep learning curve of cultivating the land, raising cows, chickens, and pigs. Failure and success intermingled, but they remained steadfast in their pursuit of a dream far removed from the big city.

ᒧᕈᕽᕲ

What does this parallel coming-of-age have to do with Mike and Tom's future work for community change?

These were not easy years for dairy farmers, if indeed such a thing exists. The meager price farmers got for their milk was so low that it seemed every time they went to the barn in the predawn hours to milk, they left the barn deeper in debt. And in the evening, when they did it again, they went even deeper in debt, until finally the banker called them in and told them the game was over: pack it up. This was in the early 1960s, when many American farmers walked away from their farms, getting pennies on the dollar. Desperation lit a fire under farmers that had laid dormant since the days their fathers and mothers had taken on the robber barons and railroad monopolies sixty

3

years earlier. They created an organization—the National Farmers Organization (NFO). The Mosgallers and the Breiningers, unknown to each other at the time, both eventually joined the NFO.

One cold March Saturday morning, 16-year-old Tom's life took an unexpected turn. His father invited him to accompany him and their neighbor, Rueben, to a "holding action" farm rally. Tom, a stranger to such events, eagerly accepted, seeing it as a rite of passage to be asked to go with the men to whatever a "holding action" thing was. Besides, anything seemed better than the usual Saturday routine of mucking out the cow barn!

As the rally drew to a close, Rueben and Tom's father joined other participants in pouring raw milk on the ground in protest of the low prices. As they were getting into their truck to leave, a fancy car with Illinois plates hurled a rolled-up newspaper in their direction, yelling "Read this you stupid farmers!"

Tom retrieved the mud-soaked newspaper and read aloud the headline: "Wisconsin Farmers Starve Chicago Children?" The words hung heavy. He will never forget the look on his dad's and Rueben's face when he handed them the newspaper. "Are we starving Chicago children?"

Rueben offered a measured response: "Tom, these issues are complicated."

That question and Rueben's response became the genesis story for Tom's commitment to learning the things they don't teach you in civics class: that preachers never explain and powerful people don't want you to know.

 ⌒〰

Mike's story, too, bears witness to a pivotal moment—one that would shape his perspective and ignite a passion for change.

One day in the late 1960s, 11-year-old Mike's dad called him into the milk house on the farm where they kept their milk before shipping. Mike had often listened at the dinner table, down at the feed mill, and after church when his dad, mom, and other farmers talked about their desperate efforts to keep their farms.

Standing there in the milk house, Mike's dad pointed to the milk tank and said, "What I am going to do is for you and the future of many other people. I don't know how we will feed ourselves, but I am going to dump our milk down the drain so you can have a better life." He leaned over and opened the valve on the milk tank and let the milk run down the drain. With big eyes, Mike watched in painful silence as every drop of milk drained from the tank, and every penny from their checking account. Mike didn't really understand all that was happening, but he knew his dad and the other farmers were doing this for him, their families, and their future.

With the backdrop of neighborhood boys starting to go off to the Vietnam War, Mike wondered if there would even be a world left when he grew up.

✺

We'd love to tell you that these Midwest farmers' desperate demonstrations of solidarity and sacrifice, like a feel-good television sitcom, ends with farmer heroes and that everyone lived happily ever after. But that would be a lie.

The farmers lacked one fundamental ingredient—the power to overcome the overwhelming resistance of the milk processing companies to negotiating with the farmers.

Many young men and women who experienced the milk strikes growing up, just like young people everywhere today who see their parents rally for causes they care deeply about, never forgot the experience. Those troubles, like seeds on good soil, became their motivation for working to leave their communities better than they found them.

∼ ⁂ ∽

For fifty years, Mike and Tom's common story went untold to each other, until in 2012 they found themselves working together on a campaign to attract young people back to rural Wisconsin communities.

The team that put this handbook together—including these two primary authors, the contributing storytellers, and the many advisors who provided feedback on its design—are all veteran community builders.

They have earned their stripes the old-fashioned way, by rolling up their sleeves and dealing with real desires and discontents, scrapes and stumbling blocks.

They have experienced the joys of success and the laments of failures but never lost their passion for building stronger communities.

∼ ⁂ ∽

So, let's get started. We have created a dynamic framework made up of critical change elements that we call the "Change Framework." The keyword is *dynamic*. Like a juggler trying to keep four plates spinning while riding a unicycle on a high wire, leading community change requires your understanding of the interdependence and interconnectedness of these elements:

- Desire (D): A strong feeling of wanting to have something or wishing for something to change, enough to lead to action.
- Vision (V): The ability to see the end before the beginning and stay focused on the vision throughout the process.
- Power (P): The ability to act.

Now, let's consider the two crucial factors that help determine your ability to act, a.k.a. your Power:

- Relationships (r): The power that comes from working with others. Strong relationships help us solve problems and support one another.
- Action (a): Doing something to achieve an aim.

Finally, community change almost always meets some kind of opposition. This can come from individuals who might have a conflict of interest in the change being proposed, a concern about unintended consequences that the change might cause, doubt about the financial viability of the change, a political or ideological problem with the change, a feeling about being surprised or left out of the initial discussions, or even a genuine misunderstanding or lack of information about what is being proposed.

We have lumped all these reactions into the word Resistance (R): A combination of factors that often (in fact, almost always) arises to community change. We are not saying that resistance is always a bad thing. In fact, sometimes it leads to great improvements in what change is being proposed; and sometimes resistance is the only viable response to truly bad ideas for change. The bottom line, however, is that the Desire, Vision, Power (relationships plus actions) always has to be greater than the Resistance if positive Community Change is going to happen.

For those of you who are mathematically inclined, the Change Framework can be expressed as a formula of seven parts:

C (Community Change) = D (Desire) x V (Vision) x P (Power) (relationships plus action) > R Resistance

1. C = Community Change
2. D = Desire (dream or discontent)
3. V = Vision
4. P = Power (the ability to act)
5. r = relationships
6. a = action
7. R = Resistance

The ultimate goal of the Change Framework is to ensure that your Desire, Vision, and Power, created by forming Relationships and taking Action, are stronger together than the forces of Resistance that will try to stop you from making positive changes in your community.

Our framework is a flexible tool that can assist any community, regardless of its size or location. This unique plan empowers people to work together, dream big, and take action to overcome challenges. Let's explore how you can use this plan to make your community a better place for everyone!

We strongly believe in the power of this framework. It's more than just a formula; it's a lifetime aspiration. Our aim is to inspire everyone in your community to dream big, collaborate, and take steps toward a brighter future. Here is a little chart that shows the elements that allow the Change Framework to succeed.

COMMUNITY CHANGE =

DESIRE ✗ VISION ✗

POWER (RELATIONSHIPS + ACTION)

> RESISTANCE

Unless you are part of a group that decided to read this book together, you are likely reading it on your own. That's how we all usually read...but it's not how we make change.

We live in a world where popular culture floods with stories of individual heroes. Scroll through the movies and series streaming today, and they are full of superheroes swooping in and saving the day (usually by beating someone up or blowing something up). Then there are the stories of the average person who just got pushed one step too far...and beat someone up or blew something up to solve all of the problems.

Most of us don't resort to violence, but too many of us have bought into the rest of the message: Change comes from one hero or leader crusading hard enough: If I argue, post, and complain enough, things will change!

Or we can jump to the opposite conclusion: I am not a crusader, lone wolf, charismatic hero, so there's nothing I can really do.

The good and bad news is this: The Change Framework is a team sport. If you want to make a change in your community, you are much more likely to succeed if you build a team. (Even the best quarterback lined up alone on a football field is pretty much doomed, even in Wisconsin.)

We encourage you to read this book with an eye to moving from "I" to "we," and then to constantly being inclined toward recruiting more people into your "we." What might that mean?

At the end of each chapter, we have an activation section that includes a "Think" activity and a "Do" activity. The Think activities are intended for you to reflect on individually and then (possibly) discuss with your group/team. The Do activities are intended for you to go beyond your group/team and engage with others.

Are you thinking, "But I don't have a group! I'm on my own"? If so, you may start out doing Think activities individually and using the Do activities to start to build your first team… and then going through the cycle again and again once you have a team.

༄

There is an inherent limitation in a book like this. Every situation is different, but the pages don't change depending on who is reading them.

Your context will shape how your efforts play out. At each stage of the process suggested in this book, your actions may look very different if you are, for example, trying to get healthy food in your school lunchroom versus trying to keep thirty families from being evicted in order that someone can build a golf course.

People are individually complicated. Groups are even more complicated. And when you get to communities, societies, and cultures, the complexity skyrockets.

Fortunately, so do the possibilities.

We didn't attempt to include stories in this book that reflect the breadth of possibilities across cultures and geographies. That would be impossible. You will notice that many of the stories come from small cities, towns, and rural areas in the Midwest. but the principles and practices apply and have been used in both urban and suburban environments as well.

And every kind of community has these stories - because people are creative, people care, and people work to make things better. Your challenge is to figure out how the Community Framework can be adapted and applied where you are.

If you read this book and think, "My community isn't represented here" or "that would never work here," we urge you not to stop reading. Think about exactly *how* your community is *different* and what *might* work *there*. The principles behind the Change Framework could happen where you live and work—if you are passionate and can work with others. We'd love to hear what you come up with. We're serious. That's why we are offering readers a way of contacting us directly and share what you are doing.

For example, we are creating a Pulling-Together workbook that will complement the handbook. It provides readers exercises/tools for working through the Change Framework in their communities. It will provide downloadable PDFs at our website Pulling-Together. com for ease of access and will provide ways readers can share their own stories of community change that we can review and then add to the website as a way of sharing the lessons they have learned.

༄

The next three pages give a little tutorial on what it takes to be or become a community leader.

**Everyone a learner
Everyone a teacher
Everyone a leader**

Rarely in life are we prepared to lead. An opportunity sparks our imagination or a heartburn happens that sends a message to our brain that we can't ignore. That spark or heartburn is the voice of love for our family, our neighbors, and our community that won't let us take a pass. We step up – we engage others.

Some may call this our conscience, a call to action, our burning-bush moment. What you call it is less important than knowing in your hearts that these are the people, here is the place, and this is the time to step up – ready or not. It could be a situation where as a parent you can't stand by and watch your kid being bullied, or see your community's well water poisoned, a feel the need for a safer neighborhood or an opportunity to improve the housing stock in your town that compels you to act.

❧

Most of us are thrown into the deep end of the pool at some point in our life. Whether you consider yourself a leader or not is less important than taking the plunge and asking others to get in the pool with you. Without them you are not a leader, you're just another powerless person down at the tap room or sitting at the weekly card game hoping someone else will do something.

We all know leaders who were thrown into the deep end. Take Moses in the Old Testament Book of Exodus, God lures him into a dialogue by a bit of pyrotechnics, using a burning bush to get his attention. God tells Moses he is the one chosen to lead the Israelites out of bondage in Egypt. Moses didn't see it coming, but he knew what it meant. It meant he was being called.

What does Moses do? He tries to negotiate his way out of leading! He presents his limitations to the Lord – says he stutters, doesn't know how to lead, is not the right person for the job. Maybe God can find someone else who is a better fit – a real leader. But God knows Moses' heart, and in the end Moses's love of his people overrides his fear. He steps up, engages others, seeks advice as needed, and leads his people to the promised land.

❧

Every leadership situation is unique, of course, but some universals endure the test of time – whether it was two thousand years ago, two hundred years ago, or two days ago. What you call yourself is less important than what your love of family, neighbor, and community compels you to do.

When the voice of love for your family, your neighbors, and your community calls you to act, what will be your answer?

❧

"But I'm not a leader…." We hear this all the time. You may have said (or thought) it yourself. You certainly wouldn't be alone.

We think, however, that this feeling comes from our society's stunted view of leadership. We tend to picture someone at a microphone orating profoundly to the multitudes; or maybe the person who runs the meeting and gives the rest of us our marching orders. The amount of tension, conflict and dysfunction in community efforts that is caused by this limited view of leadership is probably hard to overestimate. We have three questions for you:

- Do you care enough to move beyond agonizing about a problem and act to do something?
- Are you willing to reach out to other people with related concerns, listen to them, come up with ideas that work for all of you, and then pull together?
- Is the desire or discontent you feel important enough that you're willing to stick with it, even if it takes way longer than you first thought?

If you answered yes to these three questions, you have the foundation you need. There are always more leadership skills to learn, but that is the case for the most seasoned leader. If calling yourself a leader gives you hives, come up with another word. Just don't let those five little words - "But I'm not a leader" - keep you from getting started.

COMMUNITY CHANGE

CHAPTER 1

"C" IS FOR COMMUNITY CHANGE

Change: the process of disrupting what is

Here comes Edward Bear down the stairs
behind Christopher Robin,
bump, bump, bump on the back of his head.
As far as he knows this is the only way to come down stairs,
but he knows there is a better way
if only he could stop bumping and think of it.

A.A. Milne, *Winnie the Pooh*

Do you want to make life in your neighborhood, your town, or your community better? Maybe there is a nagging problem you wish would go away, or something you wish would come your way.

We all want to see positive change in our world, starting in our own communities. And the more we understand why, what, and how to make community change happen, the better the odds of it actually happening. All too often changes, big or small, die on the cutting room floor because well-intended people don't have a simple, practical way to get it done.

> Community:
> People who identify with a shared place or identity (physical or virtual)

Do not define the boundaries of community. Only you, locally, know the context in which you want to make change. It could be as simple as a stop sign on the corner or as complex as getting farmers in your watershed to use cover crops on their fields.

Change requires leadership, activators willing to take the first step, a core of people who won't allow the pursuit of perfection to become the enemy of "good enough to get started." All too often, we are afraid to take action, learn from what happens, and make adjustments to keep an issue moving forward to a successful conclusion.

～

OUT OF CRISIS

Story by Tom Mosgaller

In the 1980s, Wisconsinites faced a nightmare when dry ground, higher than normal winds, and freshly plowed fields combined to produce a "perfect storm" that galvanized our community in the middle of an already existing farm crisis.

∽≫

Our story began at 3:30 PM on an autumn afternoon as Prairie View Consolidated School bus No. 7 pulled out of the school parking lot for what should have been the beginning of its routine delivering kids home to their families. The driver, Clyde Weber, a local farmer who had worked as a part-time school bus driver for twenty-one years, knew the weather signs that signaled trouble. The wind was picking up and his gut told him the stretch of Highway 14 between Shot Tower Creek and Little Patch Road was going to be treacherous. Swirling sands, sudden dust clouds, and freshly plowed fields could turn the drive from routine to a white-knuckled nightmare in a heartbeat. Clyde knew this from experience, not because he had seen it in some movie or TV show.

Every local in Prairie View, Wisconsin, had their own story of an accident, a near miss, or their own episode of a white-knuckled nightmare driving through what became known as "the murderous mile." The issue wasn't *if* something was going to happen but *when*. Who would step up and say that enough is enough? The story of bus No.7 on that fateful day became the tipping point for local community action.

ॐ

Two years earlier, new owners from outside the community had bought the land along the lower Wisconsin River Valley to expand their statewide vegetable growing operation. Their emphasis was on productivity and profitability, and they had little experience with sandy river bottom soils much less the unpredictable winds that came down through the Wisconsin River valley.

As Clyde worked his way closer to Shot Tower Creek, he could see the brown haze on the horizon. He went through his mental checklist: slow down, turn on the headlights, activate the emergency blinkers, and calmly but firmly remind the kids to stay in their seats. Then the sun began to disappear, the wind and blowing sand continued to pummel the bus, and the louder-than-usual nervous chatter that signaled the kids' merriment of the end of a school day fell to nervous whispers as everyone on board tried to will the bus through the murderous mile. Clyde leaned over the steering wheel intently, trying to stay between the white lines that intermittently appeared on the road ahead.

Based on the accident report, at 4:10 PM bus No. 7 swerved to avoid a large tanker truck hugging the centerline. It was a jarring ride down a steep embankment into an irrigation ditch and past a big oak tree.

Some of the kids were shaken up, and many got bumps and bruises, but no one was seriously hurt. Clyde Weber was cited in the accident report as having turned what could have been a tragedy into a parents' collective sigh of thanksgiving by guiding the bus to a safe stop just before it would have crashed into a large culvert. He was, by any account, a hero.

⚜

When the kids got home and began telling their parents what had happened, the fate of bus No. 7 became the talk of the township as families and friends shared the latest Episode of the Murderous Mile.

For many, bus No. 7's near tragedy was the last straw. Everyone seemed to have a cousin, a nephew, a neighbor's kid on No. 7. Emotions were running high. Charged opinions were rapidly circulating through the community. Everyone knew it was only a matter of time before someone was going to be killed.

The question was who would bring the community together? Bar-stool philosophers wanted to confront the sheriff and demand he declare a state of emergency when winds got too high; good Samaritans wanted signs posted at both ends of the murderous mile with flashing lights that could be automatically activated when winds were high; others wanted the school district to create an alternative route when the winds became dangerous: and still others were talking about seeing if the local radio station would announce dust days to warn motorists.

One evening Jan, a local music teacher by profession and farmer's wife by marriage, a "networker" by nature, sat down at the dinner table across from her husband Dean and said, "Dean, what are

19

we going to do about this?" Dean, a man of few words, knew Jan was not asking a rhetorical question for suppertime conversation. He stopped eating, thought for a moment, looked across the table, and said, "I think this calls for the convening of the Coon Rock Yacht Club. I will call some of the leaders tonight as soon as I am done milking." Jan nodded her approval.

That was the beginning of how a crisis became the spark that brought no-till soil conservation practices to the Wisconsin River Valley.

⌘

Now, for clarification, the leaders of the Coon Rock Yacht Club are not real clubby types, much less yachters. They are farmers, rural friends and neighbors who need a good time once in a while to break up the monotony of their day jobs and add a little levity to the hard work of farming. This was all the more needed during a farm crisis, when interest rates had hit an all-time high of 13-15% and many neighbors were making hard decisions about even staying on the land.

Their regularly scheduled events included the annual Christmas caroling concert which drew hundreds of people from the region; the Farmers Open Golf Tournament, held the first day of spring at the local golf course with farmers in their barn clothes and barn yard mucking boots being honorary guests, and the horse and antique tractor-pulling exhibition in the fall of each year.

While taking on a serious issue like dealing with a dust storm was not on their regularly scheduled list, they knew someone had to get the flywheel turning. They were an unlikely but logical spark, given all the relationships they had developed over the years. Jan and Dean, Carl Pulvermacher, and a handful of other local civic leaders met and agreed it was time for them to "meet" the new neighbors who owned the vegetable growing business and figure out how they could work together to resolve the murderous mile crisis before someone was killed.

They began by writing letters to the editor of the local newspaper. The local radio station started doing interviews with kids and their parents describing their experience navigating the murderous mile. And pastors began to call for action from their pulpits. The issue was heating up.

Carl agreed to call the owners of the vegetable growing company to see if they would sit down and amicably work out a solution before things boiled over. Word spread that the Coon Rock Yacht Club was working with other local civic leaders, pastors, the school district, and law enforcement to get the meeting. Many people were skeptical about whether anyone could actually get a meeting with the new landowners. Some skeptics thought they would simply ignore the request. Others thought they might send their local manager or their attorney to defend their rights to do whatever they pleased on their land. Jan, Dean, and Carl, however, believed they could figure this out just as farmers had figured out other crises over the years. And maybe even in the spirit of the Coon Rock Yacht Club would have some fun in the process.

The important thing was they took the first action. Carl had made the call and the ball was now in the landowner's court. The action would be in the reaction.

What do *you* think happened next? That's the rest of the story.

❧

APPLYING THE ESSENTIAL ELEMENTS
OF THE CHANGE FRAMEWORK

**C (Community Change) = D (Desire) x V (Vision)
x P (Power) (relationships plus action) > R Resistance**

This story provides us with a good example of how to apply the elements of community change to a problem. In this story, it was a Wisconsin farm couple who decided they had had enough and wanted to improve driver safety on Hwy 14. The desire element of community change requires us to begin by assessing if other people (relationships) will join in pursuing the dream or addressing a discontent. Once we have determined people want to do something, we need to create a *shared* Vision and then take steps (action) that everyone in the group can agree upon.

The next question is whether we can muster enough power to actually make the change happen. That will require organizing (relationship-building) as our first fundamental step (action) to address the dream or discontent. In this "Out of Crisis" story, the first public step was to mobilize the Coon Rock Yacht Club and make sure they were on board. The second step was to have the leader of the Club call to engage the errant landowners to see if they would work with the community to improve road conditions on Hwy 14.

❧

WHAT WE HAVE LEARNED

1. Communities are going to change. It is inevitable. Whether those changes reflect your dreams or address your discontent is up to you.

2. Relationship building is the foundation upon which the power to effect community change is built. You need to have the relationships before you can act.

3. What you must do is intentionally and systematically build the trusting relationships necessary for the community to choose to change.

4. Moving a community from this is "how it has always been" to "what it could be" requires leaders with a shared vision of what is possible and a willingness to act.

THE REST OF THE STORY

When Carl made the call to the vegetable growers office to invite them to meet, he had a bit of wind at his back. The organizing committee convened by the Coon Rock Yacht Club had sent a letter requesting a meeting, along with a packet of clippings from the local papers, the transcript of some of the interviews on the local radio with the bus driver, a story by a student who had been on the bus, and a neighbor sharing her own close call on the murderous mile.

The organizing committee had agreed that their first strategy was to try and work this out amicably if possible. It worked. The owner and the local manager agreed to meet the following Monday with the understanding that the meeting was not to be a media spectacle but an honest effort to resolve the crisis. Carl made it clear that local farmers, friends, and neighbors wanted only one thing—a civil conversation to resolve the safety issues on Hwy 14. The meeting was scheduled.

On a sunny fall afternoon, twelve members of the local farmers, school district, churches, and other representatives of the community met with the owner and his local manager around picnic tables in Ben Wagner's farmyard. The issues were put on the table, stories were told, frustrations were voiced, pictures of close calls passed around, and a clear one-page outline of the request for action was shared with the new owners of the vegetable farm.

The owners quickly realized the issue was not going to go away. They knew they either cooperated or the local community would take further action. The owner agreed to immediately put in cover crops when they finished their harvesting each year and to work with the county land conservation office to develop a long-range plan to improve their soil conservation practices. The farmers and neighbors offered to work with them in any way they could to help them, including showing them what they already were doing on their own farms. The meeting ended with the landowners agreeing to meet with the residents of the area in two weeks to share their specific plan.

❧

On a Monday night in early October, the auditorium of Prairie View High School was packed with people from the surrounding school district. The community leaders representing local farmers, school board, churches, and other local civic groups laid out the story of the murderous mile. The vegetable grower and the local manager were invited to present both a summary of the work they had already started to protect their fields from further soil erosion and the establishment of a long-term conservation plan. Among the practices agreed to was that all fields would have a cover crop to reduce soil loss and that they would use no-till seeding practices in the future. The county soil conservation service agreed to continue to work with the landowners to monitor their progress.

The agreement which had been reviewed earlier in the day by local leaders was publicly signed in front of the auditorium audience. Carl also announced that the owners had agreed to join a cover-crop field day walk the coming spring to demonstrate good faith and get to know their neighbors.

Everyone in attendance that Monday night applauded the leaders who had pulled together the gathering, the students who had been on the bus No. 7 were recognized for their role in getting people to take action, and leaders of the Coon Rock Yacht Club were applauded for jumpstarting the action.

❧

This small but important set of local actions became a precipitating spark for the development of a statewide network of farmers and friends called the Wisconsin Rural Development Center (WRDC), which went on to address an array of critical rural issues over the next twenty-five years. On the list of achievements was the establishment of the Center for Integrated Agriculture at the University of Wisconsin that to this day is nationally recognized for its applied research and promotion of cutting-edge farm practices and local food promotion.

As Carl Pulvermacher said at the fall potluck of the Coon Rock Yacht Club that year, "Sometimes it takes a crisis to get us off our butts, but now that we know what we can do together, we don't have to wait for the next crisis to be good neighbors."

ACTIVATION

Moving a community from **"how it has always been"** to **"what it could be"** requires leaders with a shared vision of what is possible and a willingness to act.

THINK

1. What dream or discontent do you want to **do something about?**
2. **Why** do you want to do it? Be specific.
3. Who will **benefit** from the change?
4. Who MIGHT **resist** the change?

DO

1. Talk with a few people you know to **check their degree of interest** in the dream or discontent.
2. Check if they have an interest in **learning more** about fulfilling the dream or conquering the discontent.
3. If there is interest, **determine together** your first small action steps.
4. Take action, but **one action at a time.** Let the reaction to your action determine the next action.

DESIRE

CHAPTER 2

"D" IS FOR DESIRE

Desire: a strong feeling of wanting to have something
or wishing for something to happen

It sometimes seems that intense desire
creates not only its own opportunities,
but its own talents.

Eric Hoffer

There are three drivers in life.

First is a passion (desire), almost a fire, that will not allow us to rest in our present condition.

Second is the will to act. It must be present for us to accomplish anything of true significance.

Third is energy (motivation). This is generated when passion and the will to act intersect.

> Courage:
> Being strong in the face of what is hoped for and feared

WATERING THE NEXT GENERATION
Story by Mike Breininger

Summer was breaking out over the northern U.S. during the Memorial Day weekend of 2017. Liz Perkins was thinking about trips to the swimming pool with her young children. As soon as school was out, she had plans to have the kids at the pool to enjoy their summer fun. Her six- and eight-year-old daughter and son were becoming proficient at swimming and loved to be in the water. But there was a problem.

In the southwest Wisconsin city of Richland Center, the municipal swimming pool was not a safe place for the kids to have fun. After forty years of serving the community well, the pool had large cracks in the concrete and was losing hundreds of gallons of water daily. Many families, including Liz, made the decision to travel to nearby communities for safer and better water recreation options for their children. Richland Center was at a crossroads: does the city and community invest in a new pool or demolish the old one and fill the hole? Richland Center also has a well-cared for indoor pool with fitness equipment and racquetball courts. Was that enough to serve the community well? The bigger question: is this a community that will build and grow or is it a dying place that needs to have a funeral service for the dead pool?

⌇⌇⌇

Liz would have none of it. She wanted an outdoor pool and water recreation for her children in her own hometown. She knew it would be a big challenge, but she decided to start talking to the influencers in the community to see what could be done. Liz was a mom with a mission to change her community to be a place where children and families could stay in their own hometown and thrive. She rolled up her sleeves and started the work of reaching out to people.

After conversations with some of the Park and Recreation Board, City Council members, and the Mayor, Liz realized the prospect of a new pool for the community was more difficult than she imagined. Some of the Council members were not sure they wanted to commit the resources, since Richland Center was losing young people and the budget for the city did not have enough leeway to expect taxpayers to foot the bill for a new pool costing millions of dollars.

cy͏͏ͦ

Liz contemplated where she might find help with her vision for a new pool if the city could not do it or did not have the will to do it. She began to talk to friends and neighbors. Not the big influencers, but the people in the community who might be like her, wanting a place for their children to be able to go in the summer for fun and safe recreation. People were interested and supported Liz, but she still needed to figure out how to stir up enough motivation to take action and find people who might help her in the organizational part of a new pool coming to town.

She knew about a community development group, Southwest Partners, that was active in bringing good ideas to reality. She attended one of their executive team meetings to discover it was just a bunch of community-minded people who decided they wanted to make the community a better place for everyone. Liz decided this was the group for her. She joined the group and pitched her idea of a new pool. The SW Partners team loved the idea and wanted to join the effort. They held community meetings to discuss the plan to move ahead with a new pool. They also reached out to the City Parks and Rec. Board and some of the City Council members who were favorable.

cy͏͏ͦ

Soon the momentum of the ad hoc group was stirring confidence in everyone. Liz began to feel like it was not just her in the fight, she had allies. The ideas for the pool soon took a turn to make it an aquatic center with water features like big slides, a lazy river, and variable diving boards. Consultants were enlisted in the discussion to bring some expertise. The group crafted a design with the consultants and got some cost projections.

Yikes! Over $5 million seemed like a lot for a community of 5,000 people. Some of the people in the working group were skeptical. The Council members said there was no way the city could come up with that amount of money. But Liz knew this was about the kids and about the community, not just about money. She reasoned that there must be a way to make it work and decided to present the idea to the City Council along with SW Partners and other prominent people in the community that were in full support.

Many interested and passionate people turned out for that City Council meeting to discuss the future of the aquatic center. One Council member belabored the burden on the taxpayers and the mayor seemed ambivalent. There needed to be an inflection moment, or the project would die. Then one council member stated he could see it happen if private funds could be raised for about $2 million. Then the city could bond for the remainder of the $5 million it would cost. One of the SW Partners team members, Mick Cosgrove, stood up at the meeting to communicate what the community would do to make the new aquatic center become a reality. Not even the rest of the SW Partners team knew exactly what he was going to say, but Mick knew who was with him and what it would take to persuade the Council.

What do *you* think happened next? That is the rest of the story.

⁓

APPLYING THE ESSENTIAL ELEMENTS OF THE CHANGE FRAMEWORK

C (Community Change) = D (Desire) x V (Vision)
x P (Power) (relationships plus action) > R Resistance

This story provides us with a good example of how Desire is an essential element of creating change. Here a mother was passionate about the need for a public pool for her own kids. Her next step was to come up with a common vision and then build enough power to make that vision a reality. Liz's desire for community change came from a life experience or a deeply held belief or view. Sadly, however, the fire of passion often dies in inaction. People get fired up about an idea initially, but eventually lose that fire when they do not see a path forward. If passion is allowed to take a healthy course, it will become the will to take action.

Such passion can originate from one of the following two "D" pools to transform wishes into energy (motivation):

1. **Dreams**: what we believe can be but have not yet seen as a reality. A dream demands that "we can do better." Dreams are aspirational in that they lead us to create something that is not yet in existence.
2. **Discontentment/Dissatisfaction**: the sense of injustice or misalignment that needs correction. Discontentment may lead us to proposing a fix for something that is broken or a change in direction for something that is functioning poorly.

༄

WHAT WE'VE LEARNED

1. **Taking the time to identify the points of fire**—the things you really care about—is always a worthy exercise. It is from this desire (passion) that you identify the driving force that produces your will to act (desire)—and the energy (motivation) to carry it through.

2. **Fix your will (on a target and an endgame).** Because of your passion you want to see something actually happen. The outgrowth of this desire is developing a target and an endgame.

3. **Motivation can be a fickle friend,** however. Sometimes the will to act is there, and other times the sense of giving up is encroaching at the door. When your energy wanes, you need to remind yourself of your deep passion (desire).

4. **Desire lives in the heart.** Unlike what you might have been taught, passion is not something passive; it's something that grabs you at the source of what you care most about. In a sense, you can't *not* act.

5. **The overflow of your heart** should stir the thoughts of your mind to action. As the desire of your heart is treasured, your mind comes into alignment with it and you begin to think creatively.

Love:

Love is the well spring of the heart from which all desire for change begins.

~

THE REST OF THE STORY

What Mick Cosgrove said to the City Council was galvanizing: "Mr. Mayor, Council members, if the city will commit to bonding and reallocating to contribute their portion of the new aquatic center at $3 million, we, the people of the community, SW Partners, and all the parents who want their children to enjoy water recreation here in Richland Center, will raise the other $2 million. You can count on us." Mick could only make this statement because he knew the relationships he had built with people who were committed with him to carry this effort to completion.

Liz wanted to jump off her seat in excitement, but she knew the decision still must be made by the Council. Liz or one of the SW Partners Executive Team had personally spoken with five of the eight council members. They said they would support the project only if it would not significantly raise taxes. The other two council members thought it was foolish to build a new outdoor pool when the city already had a very nice indoor pool. The Council debated for about twenty minutes until the vote was called. The room was tense as the roll call vote was taken. The "no" votes were the first to speak so there was a 3-0 margin against. Then the "yes" votes began to sound off until the measure passed 5-3!

ॱৣ৵৹

The pro-pool community group leaders met the next night to strategize about how to raise the money. It helped to have some people involved who had raised community funds in the past. There were also a couple of prominent businesspeople in the group who thought the business community would buy in if they could see that it would help them retain people in the community and generate more business. The community group did a relational mapping exercise to see with whom they needed to build relationships in order to make this happen. After the "who we *must* have," "who we *want* to have," and "who it would be *nice to* have" were determined, the group identified those they already had relationships with and those they would need to go build new relationships with. They crafted discussion points and commitment forms and sent the entire team to work.

Over the next few months, an opposition community group arose. Most of these folks were concerned that their taxes would skyrocket if this new aquatic center was constructed in Richland Center. Some thought it was foolhardy to build such a facility since they were convinced few people would use it and the operational costs would sink the city into financial ruin. One prominent landlord attended several city council meetings to voice his opposition. Each time he was allocated five minutes but went on for 40-45 minutes ranting about how stupid it was to build this aquatic center. The council was a bit intimidated and let him go on well after his time elapsed. Another oppositional community group began to post statements on social media and tried to persuade the council to rescind their vote.

ॱৣ৵৹

Liz and SW Partners, along with their many allies, however, were also hard at work painting the vision and asking people to join the effort to build a new aquatic center. The team sponsored fundraising events such as an adult prom, a golf outing, wine walks, a contributor's wall of honor, and many other visibility projects. They spent their free time talking to community members, businesspeople, and foundations who might be willing to help raise the $2 million that they had promised. They devised ways people could give at varying levels and still feel like they were part of building the new aquatic center. They found small and large businesses who committed not only to contributing money but also to donate their products and services. (In the end, in-kind contributions amounted to nearly 25 percent of the needed $2 million.)

In less than six months, the community group accomplished what seemed impossible. They were able to raise $2.1 million in cash, pledges, and product and service donations. There was a victorious presentation to the city council from a community majority that said, "Yes! We *will* build the aquatic center, and our community, for the future."

༄

At the grand opening of the new aquatic center, there was Liz standing next to the Mayor, the City Council members, the Park Board President, and engineers and builders. Few people knew that Liz had such a significant hand in making this community transformation a reality. The mayor got to make his public victory speech and others took most of the credit, but those who worked the effort knew that it was the community members like Liz, SW Partners, and the others who built the relationships and raised the funds were the real reason the new aquatic center was built in Richland Center.

The aquatic center has been a far greater draw—not only from people in Richland Center but also all-over Southwest Wisconsin—than anyone could have guessed. There was concern about being able to hire enough lifeguards, so a training program was created to help lifeguards become certified. Now there are more than enough lifeguards. The aquatic center is also a draw for new families coming to the area. The administrator of the hospital says he takes all the new doctor recruits with children to see the aquatic center. Even the man who was most vocally against the aquatic center has blended into the background since there has been little effect on his taxes.

Through the development of the aquatic center and several other significant projects initiated by community members, Richland Center is now a place that is optimistic and moving in a direction that makes people want to live there. Whether recreational opportunities, business expansions, or community celebrations, this community is a place where people can raise families, enjoy life, and work together to make things better.

ごグつ

Afternote: Within two years after the completion of the aquatic center, Liz Perkins was promoted in her professional role from a long-time kindergarten teacher to the dean of students at the high school. The following year, she accepted the position of high school co-principal. Now everyone knows what she is doing to transform the public high school. She has affectionately become known as "Aqua-Girl" for her strong role in bringing the aquatic center to reality and shifting the mindset of an entire community.

ごグつ

ACTIVATION

Taking a desire from a "wish" or a "discontent/dissatisfaction" to "energy" or "motivation" to a **"commitment or plan of action"** requires the development of a vision for your community and the power to help bring it about.

THINK

1. What are some **long-term passions** of your life related to your community?
2. What would it take for your own passion(s) to become **real desire for community change** that leads you to a will to act?
3. What might you need to **declutter in your life** so that your deepest desires can emerge? Is there one or more desires that already exist in you?
4. What might be **one or two steps** you could take to move your desire forward?

DO

1. Explore common interests and passions that your community members share. Recognizing shared passions can help **unite the community around common goals.**
2. Reflect on how these shared passions can evolve into **collective desires that might motivate the community** to take action together.
3. Identify any barriers within the community or in individual lives that need to be addressed to **allow shared desires** to surface and flourish.
4. Connect with the community's shared desires that **align with your own values and aspirations.**
5. **Envision concrete actions and strategies** that could allow you to work collectively with other community members to make shared desires a reality.

VISION

CHAPTER 3

"V" IS FOR VISION

Vision: the ability to see the end before beginning
and stay focused on the ultimate goal throughout the process

Where there is no vision,
the people perish.
Proverbs 29:18a

(King James Version)

How is vision developed and carried forward?

First, an inspiration point, a specific desire, is experienced as a place to start your vision. Then someone or some small group develops an end point or "new reality" and begins working backward. In fact, defining the outcome—not solving the problem—is the starting point of the vision creation process. For example, if the roads are full of potholes and difficult to drive on, what would be the outcome we would like to see?

THE INSPIRATION POINT

To find the inspiration point requires a few steps. For best results, this should be done in collaboration with a small group of people with the same desire. Collectively imagine what a good outcome might look like. Contemplate and let your minds think about possibilities. Try to get the picture of the ultimate outcome on a piece of paper and only then describe it in words.

There may be a need for some basic research done in order to understand outcomes that might be realistic. If we look back at the example of potholes in the road, research may include learning the cost of repair or replacement and what best-conditioned roads are like and why. The research for the actual process of repairing or replacing the road would take place later. For now, it is a vision—but already it is not *just* a vision.

Attempt to identify the scope of the vision. In the road repair example, determine specifically what roads will be part of the repair effort and which roads will not. Start with a rough draft, but then have some good editor help craft each word so anyone can read and understand what the vision is about. Now the end point of the vision exists. Now you can begin to fill in the steps of the vision.

THE INFLECTION POINT

The inflection point is when there is a tipping or change. An inflection in a vision happens when enough resources and information are gathered that the focus shifts from accumulating resources to a major focus on action. This might be described as the transition from the gathering phase to the action phase.

THE GATHERING PHASE

This phase requires the most important resource to be collected: The People (a.k.a. your supporters). The most important resource to make a vision a reality is usually people. People are needed for their commitment, talent, and leadership. In order to understand who is needed, it's helpful to engage in what we call "relational mapping." Relational mapping can be broken down into these categories:

1. **People we must have** on board with the vision. This will usually be the leadership people and the go-to people to get things done. These people will carry the vision and help implement it when needed.
2. **People we want to have** but are not vital to the completion of the vision. Want-to-have people are those who might influence others or offer expertise that would be useful.
3. **People it would be nice to have.** These are people in the community that may not add much labor or vision but can increase the totality of numbers and momentum to the change.
4. **People who may resist the vision** are people that require strategic engagement and relationship building so that they won't resist what is being accomplished. These folks might be government officials or strategic citizens that can make or break the vision moving forward.

The Tangibles. The tangibles are the material resources that must be gathered to make the vision a reality. This might be money or a place to meet or contributions from those producing something that will aid in the vision being accomplished. It is a challenge to gather the required tangibles early in the change process because people who might contribute are looking for something that demonstrates this action will happen. A successful track record by an individual or an organization is helpful, but the most important ingredient for gathering resources is relationship with the contributor. Build the relationships, cast the vision, show that it is more than just talk, and resources will likely follow.

The Intangibles. An area that is often missed by people trying to change their community is the need for the goodwill of the community to be in support of the change. This is an immaterial resource that is measured by people's desire to join what is being proposed. The vision must be crafted so as to invite people to join themselves emotionally and intentionally to the goodwill action. If the action is seen as self-serving or against something, the goodwill may not be built to make it happen. Intangibles include things like radio spots, TV, internet advertising, and personal testimony at public gatherings (City Council, County Board, Service Clubs, Youth Centers).

ᔧᔮᔡ

MY HOMETOWN HAS REIMAGINED ITS FUTURE

Story by Jeff Yost

My hometown, Red Cloud, Nebraska, where I grew up, thought it had seen its best days decades ago. Outmigration, consolidation of farms, loss of local businesses, and a general malaise had taken hold. What could be done?

In 1950, Red Cloud had 1,744 residents; in 2023 it had 998. When my twenty-two classmates and I graduated from the only high school in 1986, it was the height of a farm crisis devastating small towns. The implicit message to me and everyone my age was: If you're a bright kid with ambition and talent, your future is somewhere else.

Many of us, literally and figuratively, received suitcases for graduation. Parents talked with pride about their kids in Lincoln, Omaha, Kansas City, or Denver. Young people who moved back to Red Cloud after college were sometimes asked, with little apology, "What happened? Couldn't you make it in the big city?"

I guess I was different. I remain deeply connected to my hometown. My 92-year-old mother, who recently passed away, lived there her whole life. Two of my sisters reside in Red Cloud. A brother and his husband have restored an historic home for a second residence. My kids know Red Cloud well.

In the 1990s, when I was in my twenties, I had many conversations with local leaders about economic development. Many wanted to recruit an ethanol plant for the town. I suggested that would be difficult, as Red Cloud would struggle with poor transportation logistics, pending water use restrictions, and because most corn raised in the area was already being used for feeding cattle.

On the other hand, Red Cloud has always had an incredible community asset. It is the childhood home of Pulitzer Prize-winning author Willa Cather. Six of Cather's twelve novels are based here, and twenty-two nationally designated historic buildings and sites related to Cather are in or near Red Cloud. This is more local acclaim than for any other American author. At least 8,000 Cather enthusiasts take a pilgrimage to Red Cloud annually.

Unfortunately, most of these visitors didn't spend the night or even have a meal. What would happen if the community invested in this one-of-a-kind cultural treasure? Could heritage tourism become a new economic engine for Red Cloud?

This question became one of two primary areas of emphasis for the Red Cloud Community Foundation Fund. This group of eight community volunteers decided they wanted to learn more and asked the statewide Nebraska Community Foundation to help investigate.

We knew additional tourism would diversify the agriculturally based economy, but we learned this heritage tourism opportunity could be especially lucrative because most Willa Cather enthusiasts tend to be well-educated and financially better-off than the average tourist. Maybe they would respond to a unique and comprehensive experience that they could only get here. In 2013, the Red Cloud

Community Fund provided a $20,000 grant to study this question: How do we get more—possibly substantially more—visitors to Red Cloud, and how do we get them to spend an extra day, a long weekend, or even a week in Red Cloud and Webster County?

⟲⟳

The economic impact study yielded some eye-popping results. If there were a significant expansion of lodging options, more dining options, and new services such as guided tours, picnics on the prairie, and other experiential opportunities, then some 3,500 visitor couples from outside the local area might stay multiple days, spending an average of $1,000 per couple per trip. This could mean $3.5 million of new economic activity, which could lead to an economic impact on Red Cloud of nearly $6 million per year. This could generate seventy-seven new jobs and over $100,000 of new local sales and lodging tax revenue annually.

Local leadership took notice and action. First, a multi-year commitment (from a coalition of local funders) was made to fully underwrite the position of Heritage Tourism Development Director. Jarrod McCartney, a Red Cloud High School alum, has now been in place for nine years. Red Cloud is flourishing. Since 2015, forty-one new businesses have started, and nineteen downtown building and tourism improvement projects have been catalyzed. City sales tax receipts have increased 56%. Among the new downtown amenities are a wine bar, a bicycle rental shop, dance studio, new coffee shops, more restaurants, and several second-story residential units. Numerous bed-and-breakfasts now operate.

Former First Lady Laura Bush spoke at the dedication in 2017 of the $7.3 million National Willa Cather Center. Red Cloud was named to the "15 Best Small Towns to Visit in 2023" by *Smithsonian Magazine*. In early 2025, The Hotel Garber opens a 27-room boutique hotel designed to appeal to Willa Cather enthusiasts. This $9 million investment will further transform downtown into the destination envisioned in the study.

༄

APPLYING THE ESSENTIAL ELEMENTS OF THE CHANGE FRAMEWORK

C (Community Change) = D (Desire) x V (Vision) x P (Power) (relationships plus action) > R Resistance

This story provides us with a good example of how vision is an essential element of creating change.

Here was a young man deeply connected to his hometown and his family who questioned the conventional wisdom held by many residents about the future and searched for alternatives that might help the community prosper. He eventually recruited other leaders in the community, who together formed a community foundation that came up with a shared vision and built enough power through their relationships to bring about positive change. Trust and teamwork were the essential elements of helping the potential opportunities they identified become actionable.

WHAT WE HAVE LEARNED

1. **Vision sets the course.** The vision is what conceives the outcome, what allows the focus in moving forward—where we are heading and what we expect for the outcome. The vision also sees at least some of the checkpoints or possible hurdles along the way. In crafting a course forward, it is vitally important to have vision and stay in the lane of that vision.

Vision lets us remember what we are hoping for as the outcome.

2. **A vision and a dream are not the same thing.** Vision is where ideas meet reality. Dreams are expressions of inmost wants and desires. Some dreams will never encounter reality, but a vision must always be framed in true-world engagement. That does not mean that dreams never become reality; it means that dreams must become a vision with substance and focus in order for us to be able to achieve the change we desire.

3. **Vision needs to have a clear endpoint.** A vision is the outcome the group is hoping and expecting to happen. As the vision is being carried out, of course, a greater understanding of what people and resources are necessary to make the good idea become reality develops.

4. **The clearer the vision, the more likely people will be drawn to it.** A well-crafted and articulated vision will be expressed in a way that is attractive and aspirational. Someone should be able to hear or read the vision in less than five minutes and have a good understanding of what the project is about. Vision is what makes people willing to put their precious time and resources into making the change we want to become the reality we live.

5. **There will be challenges—but vision will carry the day.** Some challenges may include opposition from people in the community, governmental, media, or other organizations. Do not underestimate the power of "not in my back yard," a.k.a. "NIMBY." If your supporters are conflict-avoidant, they will be tempted to run and hide as soon as there is strong opposition. So they must be reminded often, but especially when being challenged, of the vision and ultimate end point so they are able to stand up to opposition and keep moving forward.

6. **Vision creates a point of reference.** People sometimes have "mission drift" that takes them outside their stated purpose and direction. Or sometimes they get distracted by what we call "a bright shiny object." Reminding your followers of the vision often helps reduce distractions and make the vision more alive and real to them.

7. **Vision is more compelling than any person**, no matter how charismatic he or she might be. In carrying out the work of change, people sometimes change their minds or want to change the vision to make it more in line with their personal views. Keeping the collective vision before everyone will help your people continue if others drop out or become discouraged.

8. **Vision must build something.** Sometimes plans are made that include the need to tear down what is perceived as destructive. Without a clear vision of an aspirational outcome, however, vision is unsustainable. Tearing down cannot be the vision, it can only be one necessary step in the process of building something new and substantial.

❧

THE REST OF THE STORY

Simultaneously with the economic Willa Cather initiative, some local leaders (specifically Sally Hansen and Ashley Armstrong) also focused on a strategy for keeping current residents and attracting new ones: early-childhood education. Sally, Ashley, and many more early-childhood advocates in and around Red Cloud knew they needed to help their fellow community members better understand why having high-quality, affordable, early-childhood education is important for every child, every family, and every community.

In laypeople's terms, early-childhood education is critically important because: (1) ninety percent of brain development occurs in the first five years of life; and (2) children learn to love, trust, and empathize by the time they're 18-months-old. Therefore, a community can't wait for education to begin in kindergarten; it needs to provide as much education as it can, as soon as it can, for every child.

To build this understanding, Sally, Ashley, and their crew decided to have lots of individual and small group conversations. Simultaneously with the heritage tourism initiative, they had sixty-two separate community meetings with any group that would meet with them. Formal or informal. A knitting club. The VFW. A bank board. A coffee klatch. A Farm Bureau meeting. The Lions Club.

This group pursued any opportunity to help their fellow community members understand that, in the twenty-first century, ordinary childcare (which is mostly focused on safety) isn't adequate. If people in Red Cloud want to live and work in a world-class community, they must have early-childhood education available to all children. That was the vision.

All of these conversations and community meetings paid off. In 2018, The Valley Child Development Center (TVCDC)—a 7,200 square foot, $2.1 million state-of-the-art facility—opened to provide education and care to eighty children. This has made Red Cloud a hub for working parents for miles around.

And the timing proved fortuitous. Because TVCDC was opening, a Red Cloud High School alum and her husband agreed to purchase the only grocery store in town. At the time, the couple had three young children and early-childhood education was non-negotiable for their family. Hometown Market is now a cornerstone of downtown Red Cloud.

All of this visionary work is having the desired effect. Leaders in Red Cloud took this saying to heart: *Leaders are people who create a shared vision powerful enough to lift people out of their day-to-day petty preoccupations and focus them on things worthy of their effort.*

♪

I'm incredibly proud of my family and friends who are reimagining Red Cloud. This community-building work has taken years of patience, persistence, and teamwork. Today more tourists are visiting and staying longer. Early-childhood education is a given. So is the grocery store.

Residents now talk with pride about Willa Cather and how exciting it is to have a vibrant downtown. Through the Red Cloud Community Fund, residents and alumni are investing in the community through current and estate gifts. Entrepreneurship is now the economic development focus.

At the most recent Alumni banquet, speakers mentioned how impressed they are with Red Cloud and how it has reimagined itself. Most importantly, parents and local leaders are now giving high school graduates copies of Willa Cather novels, not luggage, and inviting them to make Red Cloud their hometown for generations to come.

ACTIVATION

Finding and encouraging people to develop a passion and a vision for the future of their own town or area **begins with you.**

THINK

1. Create a vision for your community, **starting with the end point.** Do so individually and then recruit a small group to think about the ultimate goal for your shared vision.
2. Create **intermediate inspiration points** that could help spread your vision and desired outcome.
3. Create an inflection point. What will be **the sign for the group** that it is time to say, "yes" and fully commit to carrying out their vision?

DO

1. Group activity: Using the four circles in the graphs below, identify the people *you must have* on your side to carry out your vision. Put them in the center circle. Relationships must be built with most if not all these people.

2. Identify the people *you want to have* in the vision and put their names in the second concentric circle. Relationships will need to be built with many of these people.

3. Identify the people it would be *nice to have* so they can be supporters when you need them and general community influencers. Add them to third circle.

4. Now identify people who *may resist your vision* for your community and put them in the outer circle. How can relationships be built with some if not all these people so they will not be a hindrance to your vision?

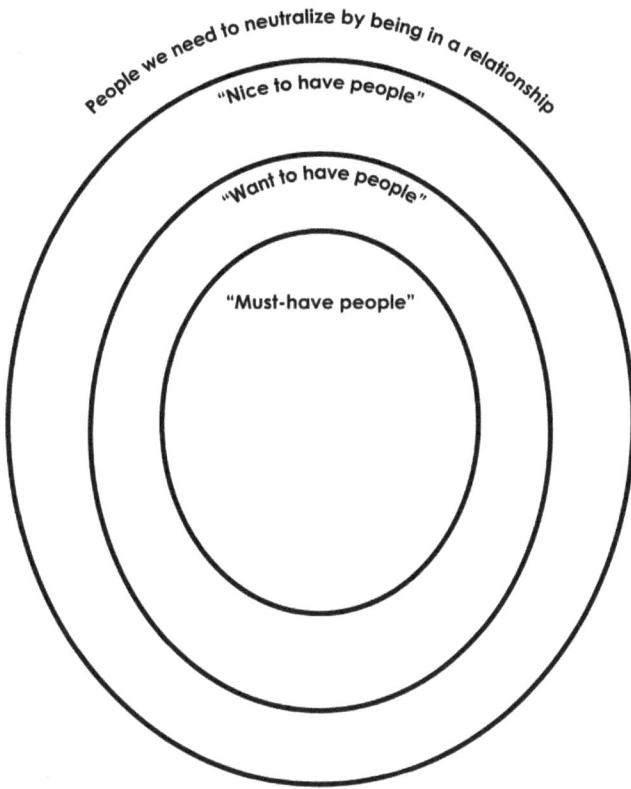

POWER

CHAPTER 4

"P" IS FOR POWER

Power: the ability to act from the Latin root verb *posse,*
meaning "to be able" or 'to make possible"

To be alive is power,
Existing in itself,
Without a further function,
Omnipotence enough.

Emily Dickinson

W̲e all have some power. It may be physical, intellectual, emotional, spiritual, economic. It can be individual, familial, tribal, constitutional. It is our birthright as human beings or (in religious terms) as children of God or (in political terms) as members of a political entity.

Few of us, however, find our footing well enough to optimize our potential for power, much less understand why exercising it is important. Power is the engine that propels our desire for change and the vision of what the world could be into results in the service of the common good. It is power that allows community change to be *posse* in Latin (possible in English).

If "abuse" of power is a sin, maybe we should also consider "the lack of use" of our power to be a sin of omission. For if we fail to use the power we do have to realize the things we could have done something about for the common good, isn't that just as bad an using our power to maintain the status quo that is preventing the common good to come to realization?

When we look at our change formula below, power "P" becomes the generator that turns our desire "D" and our vision "V" into building the relationships and taking the action necessary to get things done. Without power, our desire and vision become pipe dreams that not only prevents community change from happening but also encourages others to wallow in their apathy and the belief that "you can't fight city hall."

Power
 The ability to act.

60

THE POWER OF DISABILITY
Story about Judy Heumann, as told by Kristen Joiner

"I never wished I didn't have a disability," Judy Heumann told me in our first interview. I was a non-profit executive director turned writer, lucky enough to have been asked to co-write Judy's memoir. Our interviews would stretch out over the entire next year, but those eight words she'd uttered so early in our process stuck in my brain: *Judy never wished she wasn't disabled?*

From *Star Wars* to *Me Before You*, nearly every Hollywood movie tells us that becoming disabled is worse than dying. What is it that made Judy different? And what gave her the courage to be a part of leading the events that ended up literally changing the physical landscape of the United States?

◦୬ଡ଼ଚ

Judy was a quadriplegic due to a bout with polio at eighteen months. As a child, she used a manual wheelchair to play with the other kids on her Brooklyn block. She grew up in a close-knit German-Jewish family in a time that viewed disability as a sign that someone in the family had done something wrong. At that time, Brooklyn—like the rest of the country—was a locked box for anyone with a disability. There were almost no curb cuts from sidewalks to streets, few accessible buses or planes or bathrooms, limited ramps into restaurants, classrooms, libraries, churches, or college campuses. The status quo for disabled children and adults at that time was institutionalization, which is what Judy's doctor had recommended when she was a baby. But Judy's parents refused. They'd escaped Nazi Germany as teenagers and lost their parents and grandparents to the Holocaust; their little daughter wasn't going anywhere.

As a kid, however, Judy didn't know any of this. All she knew was that on what should have been her first day of kindergarten, she got to pick out her favorite dress and walk to school with her mother, ready to start class with all her friends on the block. But an hour later, Judy was sent home in tears. The principal had intercepted them in the hallway to let them know that disabled kids were not allowed in school.

So for the next four-and-a-half years, Judy stayed home with her mother and baby brother and watched her younger brother and her two best friends walk to school every day without her. Her childhood could be characterized by one lie: You don't belong.

✺

Over the years, however, Judy's parents, continued to push the school district to get Judy into some type of formal education. At age nine, she was allowed into a very limited special education program. The class, which was segregated in the basement of a "regular school," ranged in age from eight to seventeen. Despite their age, the older students were forced to nap every day and some had never learned to read. It soon became clear that none of the teachers seemed to expect the students in the special class to learn anything beyond what they would need to enter a sheltered workshop at eighteen.

But Judy felt that she'd found her place. She loved making friends with the other students and, for the first time in her life, discovered peers that shared her experience of the world. Their conversations helped her put into words feelings that she'd had for a long time but never spoke. "We spent hours," she told me in one of our many Zoom sessions, "trying to figure out why we were treated so differently from the kids upstairs. We talked about our [nap time] and wondered why we had to have it, since it just took time away from learning."

The students shared feelings of being extraneous, dismissed by a society that never even gave them a chance to fail, much less to succeed. At that same time, Judy knew she were learning something essential that would become critical to her future achievements. "I learned we all had something to contribute," she told me. "Steve was a jokester; Neil was great at math; Nancy was a loving friend with a beautiful smile; and I loved feeling useful."

⌁

Against all odds, Judy went on to high school and eventually graduated from Long Island University. This despite the inaccessibility of the campus, which required her to ask a classmate for help up or down the stairs every time she wanted to go to the bathroom or enter a classroom. All the while, she continued making friends. She joined a sorority, ran for junior class secretary, and joined the disabled students association. After college, with all the credentials necessary for becoming a New York City public school teacher, she applied for her license. But at the routine medical exam, required of every teaching applicant, the doctor asked her to physically demonstrate how she went to the bathroom. (A question clearly out of the bounds of any normal medical exam for anyone.)

Judy was humiliated. She stared at the doctor, holding back hot, angry tears. Finally, she said she would do what he asked "only if all teachers were going to have to show their students how to go to the bathroom." When three months later she learned that the doctor had determined she was unable to teach and the Board of Education had denied her license due to her paralysis. Judy was upset all over again. But she was not surprised.

The key to this story is what Judy did next.

⌒⌇⌒

APPLYING THE ESSENTIAL ELEMENTS OF THE CHANGE FRAMEWORK

C (Community Change) = D (Desire) x V (Vision) x P (Power) (relationships plus action) > R Resistance

The use of power, rightly understood, as a leader, an organization, a network is essential to a healthy process of community building.

The opposite of power isn't powerlessness, it is apathy, the unwillingness or inability to take action. Power is rarely talked about in everyday conversation, yet it is all around us. Most of our information these days comes through headlines, tweets, texts, or TikTok—most of which highlight the negative uses of power rather than the positive potential of using power for good.

For purposes of our formula for community building, we are framing our use of power as having two ingredients: building relationships and the willingness to act. We call this "power with" and contrast it with the dominant narrative of "power over." When we truly understand power as our ability to act on the things we love and care about, it fundamentally transforms how we lead, organize, and act in a democratic society. The more relationships we build and actions we take together, the more our trust and trustworthiness quotient increases and, like a flywheel, it becomes more powerful in the pursuit of what we all care about.

Power Analysis:

A power analysis is simply a tool to help you assess the amount of power you have to do the things you want to get done in your community. It can be used by an individual leader or as a group exercise. A power analysis helps you map out:

- Who could help make your plan a success? (Internal)
- Who has the power to help make the changes you are seeking? (External)
- Who might oppose your plan? (Opponents)
- What questions do you still need to answer?

WHAT WE HAVE LEARNED

1. Power is morally neutral. It can be used for good and/or evil. It is a means (**often a necessary and sometimes the only means**) to achieving the ends we desire.

2. In a democratic society there are **two primary forms of power: organized people and organized money.**

3. Understanding the difference between power over (dominant power) and power with (relational power) **defines how we act and how we feel** about what we accomplish and how we accomplish it.

4. Power is **not readily shared by those who are exercising it.** It has to be earned. Often it has to be demanded.

5. Power is **not finite. Nor is it linear.** It can grow exponentially through the relationships we build and the actions we take.

6. Usually there are three stages of building power. We call them **"The Three R's."** (And we don't mean Readin', 'Ritin', and 'Rithmetic!") They are:

   A. **Recognition:** This means those with power in a particular situation **need to know who we are—not just as individuals but as an organization.** As with the old story of the farmer who first had to hit his mule upside the head just to get his attention before he could gently get the mule to pull his wagon, so too do we sometimes have to "fight" just to get recognized.

   B. **R-E-S-P-E-C-T:** Recognition, although essential, is never enough. **Organized people are often** paid lip service but **not taken seriously.** This is usually to see if they are simply going away or maybe don't care that much about what they are pushing or protesting. And that tactic works more often than you think. Respect comes from and produces what we call "mutual accountability." That is, both sides of an issue make promises and agreements that the other side can hold them to.

C. **Results:** This is **how we really know that we have power.** Did the new corporate farm owners keep their word and become good citizens of the community, did the new water park get built and maintained, did the town and then the state develop a whole new strategy for tourism, did people with disabilities get their rights?

THE REST OF THE STORY

Judy got on the phone and called her disabled friends. She had already shared with them her experience with the doctor, and they'd all been expecting that she might be denied her license. All of her friends had stories of being warned away from careers and opportunities that weren't considered "realistic" for people with disabilities. They encouraged her to fight the ruling. But Judy was insecure and uncertain. How could she stand up publicly and demand the right to teach when she had never taught before? What if she failed? Her friends rallied around her. Didn't she have as much right to try and fail as any other twenty-two year old?

Her friends saw her cause as their collective cause. They'd always been told that their disability was the reason they couldn't have access to this school, that bus, or that opportunity, but they refused to see it that way. For them, being disabled in any way is a simple fact of being human, and they felt that society should be designed to be accessible for all humans. Judy's case could be a specific example that could raise awareness of all of their issues. The group had almost no money, very limited ways to even get to a protest, and society saw them only as a burden, but they had one another. Their support gave Judy strength and courage.

If I don't fight, who will? she thought.

⟡

Judy began networking. She called a disabled acquaintance from college who was a stringer for *The New York Times*. They called another mutual friend. An article came out. Then another. A well-known lawyer read one of the articles and volunteered to represent Judy in court. Within very little time, Judy had a lawyer and a case. Her friends and their wheelchairs took up the entire back row of the courtroom. (Yes, they found a bus they could all access.) The judge ordered the school district to resolve the issue, and Judy was invited to re-do the medical exam. This time, with a different doctor, she passed the exam and received her license to teach in the New York City School System. Judy's old school—the school, where she'd been placed as a nine year old, never expected to go to college—offered her a job that was responsible for teaching both disabled and nondisabled students. Judy Huemann became the first teacher with a disability that any of those students had ever had.

At the same time, Judy and her friends decided to use the energy mobilized by her court case to start an organization that would be run by and for people with disabilities. They called it Disabled in Action.

Disabled in Action worked on many of the issues that affect disabled people from ending sheltered workshops and institutionalization to fighting for accessible transportation. In 1972, about two years after launching the organization, Judy and her friends, who were tracking policy in the U.S. Congress, noticed a tiny section written into a new governmental rehabilitation bill: It was Section 504. Section 504 proposed to protect disabled people from being excluded from any program or activity funded by the U.S. government. If the bill passed with Section 504 intact, the bill would change everything for people with disabilities.

❧

To support the bill, Disabled in Action decided they needed allies. Traditionally, the disability community was divided by the nature of people's disabilities. For example, the deaf community, the blind community, the Vietnam War veterans, and so on all had their own separate advocacy organizations. Disabled in Action reached out to these groups and proposed they work together to get Congress to pass Section 504 with enabling regulations that would give it teeth.

Once united, they strategized together, gave congressional feedback together, and advocated together for over four years. Section 504 passed in 1973 but remained without enabling regulations until 1977—when Judy and her friends led the longest sit-in in U.S. government history— and they finally succeeded. The regulations were finally signed on April 28, 1977— turning Section 504 into the transformative law it remains today.

❧

This is one concrete example of how change happens in America. The entire landscape of the country was re-shaped. All entities now receiving federal funding are now required to be accessible to people with disabilities, including airports, airplanes, buses, government and social service agencies, and public transportation.

Thirteen years later, in 1990, this broad coalition of individuals and organizations that Judy had helped form and lead would play a significant role in achieving the passage of the American Disabilities Act that continued what Section 504 had started by guaranteeing people with disabilities the same opportunities as everyone else in almost every venue.

Later, much later, Judy would write this in her memoir, *Being Heumann:* "Change never happens at the pace we think it should, it happens over years of people joining together, strategizing, sharing, and pulling all the levers they possibly can. Gradually, excruciatingly slowly, things start to happen, and then suddenly, seemingly out of the blue, something will tip."

ACTIVATION

Below find some "think" and "do" activities to help you **deal with your own understanding and feelings** about power.

THINK

1. How do you react to this famous saying about power by Lord Acton, an English Catholic lay leader long ago: **"Power tends to corrupt, and absolute power corrupts absolutely."** (P.S. He was referring to the Vatican, not the British monarch at the time.)
2. Do you have enough power to effect the change you are seeking? E.g., enough or the right **relationships, allies, knowledge, financial resources?**
3. Do you have a core team of leaders? **What are their names?** Are they really with you? How can you find out?

DO

1. Bring together your core team and **do a "power analysis"** of those individuals and institutions that members of your group already have relationships with and those whom you still need to build relationships with. (Be sure to include your existing allies on the map, including yourselves!)
2. What is the power analysis **telling you?**
3. What will be your next steps to broaden and deepen your relational power **before getting into action?**

RELATIONSHIPS

CHAPTER 5

"r" IS FOR RELATIONSHIPS

Relationship: the melding of two or more people
around their mutual self-interests

Habit is habit
and not to be taken lightly
but brought down the stairs
one step at a time.

Mark Twain

Change happens at the speed of relationships. That is a sentence you don't see in many books on change. But it is absolutely true in our formula for community change. No relationships, no action. No action, no reaction. No reaction, no recognition or respect. No recognition or respect, no results. No results, no power. No power, no community change.

Why is intentionally building relationships important to getting things done? Well, for most people, there are only two forms of exercising their power: Organizing others and (sometimes) organizing other people's money. It is only then that we can take effective action.

Of course, most of us have little money and few relationships. But we all have some, and together we can multiply our numbers and assets to have enough power to be heard.

So, if we want to effect community change, we have to begin with building relationships. That is what this chapter is about, and here is a story that illuminates it.

Relational Power:
The power that comes from working with others.

BUILDING RELATIONSHIPS BEFORE YOU TAKE ACTION

Story by Michele Engh

I once met a widow with a three-year-old child, living in Vernon County, Wisconsin. Before heading to work, she used to drive to a neighboring community thirty-three miles away to drop her child off, return to her community to work, and then drive the sixty-six-mile round trip to pick up her child. Daily, she traveled 132 miles to ensure her child could be cared for while she worked. A local hospital system administrator once told me that recruiting medical professionals is often difficult purely due to the lack of regulated childcare in the community. One school district I know buses the pre-school children of their teachers to a childcare program in another district to keep the teachers able to teach in their district.

These stories are not unusual, at least in rural Wisconsin.

❧

My children are now grown, and childcare was not on my radar until I was employed by the county where I still live to address economic development. I thought the solution was simple: Just build

75

and staff a new childcare center of some kind. That would certainly bring about economic development!

But then I spoke to the head of a local not-for-profit childcare agency, who shared with me that to be financially successful they needed over 100 children enrolled in any facility they built in order to meet the licensing requirements. I realized this wasn't going to work in many small communities in rural Wisconsin. I had to learn more.

⟐

Fortunately for me, I had spent years purposefully building relationships in my community, with a focus on earning and reciprocating trust. When I met a new person, I wanted to get to know them. What drove them? What were they passionate about? Who and what do they love the most? As people talked, I found that much more unites us than divides us. So I knew what I had to do: more one-to-one relational meetings before I even proposed what might, much less should, be done in Vernon County.

I also follow through with what I say I will do. (So my next step was clear: I began a disciplined campaign of asking a lot of questions of A LOT of people. I listened to parents, childcare workers, childcare directors, employers, and childcare experts. Local childcare providers shared stories of working six days a week from 7 am to 6 pm. They had to do the shopping, the cleaning, the sanitizing, the helping with homework, the menu development, the meal preparation, and many other tasks.

Out of those conversations came the idea of the Wisconsin Early Education Shared Network (WEESSN). The idea was to offer real help to existing childcare providers by sharing as much of their non-childcare "homework" (such as invoicing, purchasing, and planning) as possible. WEESSN started with just two providers of such services and, as of today, had 2200 providers statewide.

‹⁓›

Now, that effort was wonderful and it worked, but a lot of the childcare in our community is provided by informal, unregulated providers working under the radar. One local school district even had to unexpectedly call off school for a day or so because a local, unregulated, in-home childcare provider (who was the main one that took care of schoolteachers' children) was forced to stop caring for the children in her home. Without this trusted childcare, so many teachers had to stay home from the local elementary school that students actually had to be sent home!

That is the rest of my story to come.

‹⁓›

APPLYING THE ESSENTIAL ELEMENTS
OF THE CHANGE FRAMEWORK

C (Community Change) = D (Desire) x V (Vision)
x P (Power) (relationships plus action) > R Resistance

Technology has revolutionized how we connect and build communities in our ever-evolving digital era. While social media, online forums, and virtual gatherings have expanded our reach and convenience, it's essential to recognize their limitations.

Technology undeniably offers convenience and enables connections with people worldwide. However, these virtual interactions often lack the depth of authentic in-person encounters, missing the subtleties of facial expressions, body language, and human touch. In-person meetings foster deeper connections; genuine conversations beyond superficial exchanges allow for empathy, trust, and reliability, which are essential for community cohesion.

One-to-one meetings, in particular, are instrumental in building strong community relationships. They create a safe space for open expression, active listening, and genuine support. They also facilitate conflict resolution, helping individuals find common ground and promoting open communication and collaboration, which are fundamental for community harmony. Presenting a request in person carries a more profound and more meaningful impact.

While technology has transformed community building, its true strength complements in-person interactions. One way to bridge the gap between digital and in-person interactions is to use technology to organize and promote face-to-face gatherings. Social media can be invaluable for coordinating events, contacting community members, and sharing information about in-person meetings. Social media and digital tools facilitate initial connections, but depth and authenticity thrive in personal encounters. In-person relationships provide accountability, driving individuals to pursue their goals while fostering a sense of responsibility for collective well-being. In an era of prevalent technology, we must value face-to-face interactions for nurturing resilient and thriving communities.

⌣⏾

WHAT WE HAVE LEARNED

1. Relationships are built intentionally. You have to **appreciate why relationship building is important and enjoy the habit of building them.** They are done one-to-one and

face-to-face whenever possible. By focusing your energy on building new and renewing older relationships, you both communicate and engender the energy essential to effecting the change you are seeking in your community. Relationship building is mutual. To build relationships **requires a give and take** between you and the person you are building a relationship with. It is a conversation, not a survey or an interview. You focus on listening, learning, and finding possible things you have in common. The rule of thumb is 60% listening and asking open-ended questions and 40% sharing of your own story.

2. Relationships are **built with care.** The process of relationship building is NOT experiencing a passing high-five. It is done with attention and the aim is to build trust and demonstrate trustworthiness on your part. The things that are shared in a one-to-one are kept in confidence, including that other person's stories, joys, passions, and laments.

3. Relationships are grounded in the currency of trust and forged in action. Trust is built over time, not over one cup of coffee. How we demonstrate our commitment to a relationship is through **listening, using open ended questions, learning together, and standing alongside one other.** We build currency over time.

4. We must **build relationships before you need them.** This is the hardest lesson to learn and value. Too many times we wait until there is a crisis or an opportunity that requires immediate action. We scramble to find people to join our cause rather than having networks ahead of time that can be called on based on our common interest. When you are having a fire, it is not a good time to go to the store to buy a fire extinguisher. It is much better to work at the habit of relating a little every day, every week, rather than expecting

"instant pudding relationships" when an opportunity or threat emerges.

5. Relationship building is a habit. Relationships require maintenance. Just like changing the oil in our car every 3500 miles, sustaining relationships needs to become a habit. We change, they change, the environment changes; the **ongoing process of relating, reviving, and reinventing our relationships** (including using social media) should be a living process.

The Cycle of Community Building:
　　Begin with 1-1 relationship building
　　Relational mapping
　　Building a core team
　　Research actions
　　Larger gatherings of the community
　　Evaluation/learning/getting better
　　Continue the process

THE REST OF THE STORY

When I first shared with the various school administrators and employers in two counties that we didn't have much representation from unregulated childcare providers, one of the administrators suggested that elementary school secretaries and transportation coordinators were the ones who knew where pre-school children went for care every day. Working with these school professionals, I was able to send information to unlicensed providers, using those school-staff people without violating any confidentiality. And guess what? Many of the independent childcare providers showed up to a meeting to hear what the county was proposing.

At that meeting, we listened to these unorganized childcare providers, who shared their many challenges in pre-licensing and licensing. For example, pre-licensing didn't identify needed physical modifications, which cost new providers time and money and stalled childcare programs from opening when licensers inspected their proposed premises. We also heard about the challenges childcare providers had in taking time off themselves. For them to go to a medical appointment meant closing their facility or using their backup personnel (who then had to take time off from their own employment) to run the childcare program.

꒰ᔍ꒱

WEESSN worked with the Department of Children and Families (DCF) to encourage them to better communicate with the pre-licensing agencies and the licensing agencies and to ensure a procedure for qualified-substitute providers to be able to work across multiple childcare settings. These "respite providers," as we called them, became the shared substitutes for multiple childcare providers when they need to take a planned day off. In addition, a new program for buying in bulk as a network allowed smaller childcare providers to pick up needed supplies close by versus shopping individually at a warehouse store an hour away.

The creation of WEESSN happened because of my long work of developing relationships, even before and especially after I took the job with the county. I drew upon these relationships and had to educate myself early in the process. Only then was I able to share a new vision that was built with a broad coalition of stakeholders to launch WEESSN. My relationships with school staffs, parents, and childcare providers opened the door of communication and led to them developing relationships with one another.

I continue to do one-to-ones with people on a regular basis. Sometimes they happen when we are working on something specific, but many times we meet to just catch up and enjoy a good cup of coffee. What I have discovered is that I never know when these relationships will lead to the next big effort to make our community a better place.

꒰ᔍ꒱

POSTSCRIPT

Just two weeks ago, one of the childcare centers that I had helped our community develop during this process announced their closure.

They had just joined the WEESEN shared-services, but it was too late for them to create the change they needed to survive. It is time now for us to call another meeting to try to find a solution to losing their childcare center. That will depend on pulling together the relationships that we have built in our community over the years.

And the mother who was driving sixty-six miles twice a day for her own children's care? Well, she never got to benefit from the work we did, because her own child had entered kindergarten before an opening in a community childcare ever opened up for her.

ACTIVATION

Below find some "think" and "do" activities to help you **apply the concept of one-to-one relational meetings** to your own situation.

THINK

1. What relationships do you already have? **Whom can you call this week** for a short meeting in their home or in a public place like a coffee shop or a church?
2. Who do you know who could give me some names of others I might interview? **Why would they give you the names?**

Might they even go with you on some of the individual meetings?

3. What is interesting about you? What can you share about **your life and passions** that might make others open to doing the same with you?

DO

1. Who will you call today for a meeting next week? **How many one-to-ones** are you willing to do before you even consider going into action?

2. Who else might like to learn how to do intentional relationship-building meetings? How can you share with key people whom you are meeting and what you are learning? If they are interested in learning more, **invite 2-5 together for an informal meeting.** At the meeting, practice doing one-one relationship building with your core team. What resistance do you expect? How will you deal with it?

3. After you all have done 20-30 individual meetings, bring together those people who might want to **create a "relational map"** of the key relationships you need/want before taking any action.

ACTION

CHAPTER 6

"a" IS FOR ACTION

Action: doing something to achieve an aim

Do what you can
with what you got
where you are.

Theodore Roosevelt

People often get stuck on a particular set of tactics to accomplish their goals because they may have worked for them (or others) sometime in the past. But activity masquerading as action will not get us closer to our aim. Only well-aimed, orchestrated, and continually evaluated actions improve our odds of increasing our power to achieve our desired outcome. Whenever we are going to engage in an action, it is critical to ask ourselves: *Will this particular action get us closer to this particular aim...or not?*

Moving from activity to action requires the discipline of analyzing the power dynamics embedded in the problem we are concerned about, whether it be passing a school referendum, building a new library, cleaning up the creek, or reducing reckless accidents in our neighborhood.

If you believe (like we do) that community change happens at the speed of relationships, then the intentional building of relationships through face-to-face conversations, research actions, small group gatherings, and ultimately large actions are essential building blocks of power.

Here is a story of businesspeople (specifically realtors) who made a change in their community.

> Action:
> Action is to organizations what oxygen is to you and me.

OWN IT

Story by Sarah Alvarado

Owning a home wasn't a dream of mine. It was a given, an assumed part of my future life. I'd grow up, go to college, get married, buy a home, and have kids someday. Sounds cliché, but that was the message I got, and it was my reality as a young white girl growing up in a middle-class, college-educated family. I didn't dream about owning a home one day, I dreamt only about the kind of home I'd own.

That assumption in itself is an aspect of what is often referred to as generational wealth. Even without any financial support from my family, I had a clear vision of what my life could look like as a home-owner. It was like someone being given confidence before they know they need it.

⟍⟋⟍

I got my real estate license in Madison, Wisconsin, in 2003 and was determined to become a successful realtor to help support my husband and our eighteen-month-old baby. We had just moved from Puerto Vallarta, Mexico, where I had met my husband, Carlos, a couple of years earlier. I remember getting nervous when clients would ask me where I lived. At that time, we were renting an apartment, trying to establish ourselves, and it felt inauthentic for me to be selling something I didn't even own myself, a house. But I knew it was just a matter of time for us. I knew it wouldn't be long until Carlos and I were also homeowners.

Within a couple of years, Carlos and I teamed up, and by 2008 we were the proud owners of our own real estate brokerage and our own home. For the most part, I took the ease and normalcy of homeownership for granted. On occasion, however, I'd work with clients who never thought they'd be able to own a home and experience a deep kind of a joy and excitement at the closing table as my clients signed the paperwork and received keys to their first home. That was an extraordinary feeling and it highlighted what had become normalized for me: Homeownership is (or should be) part of everyone's reality.

But, quite obviously, it is not.

In 2019, our real estate business was strong, and we had a successful sales team. Being in that position doesn't naturally call for change. What typically calls for a change is when things aren't going right, when profits are down.

It was around that time when Tiffany Malone, a realtor at a different company, invited me out for drinks eager to talk about equity, gentrification, racism, and wealth disparities. As a Black realtor in a white-dominated industry, she had a different perspective and experience than I did. The stories she shared were horrible yet not surprising. Our conversations deepened after we started reading the book, *The Color of Law,* by Richard Rothstein. We decided to gather other professionals from all different companies and lending institutions to talk about ways we could help create positive change in our community.

It was during one of these zoom meetings, in 2020, that the conversation got very specific: Down Payment Assistance Programs (DPA). Everyone thinks they are great. But they were the most complained about aspect of helping many of our clients. All the red tape and the resistance from other realtors and lenders made getting an offer with a DPA contingency accepted incredibly challenging.

Where we used to have "risky" neighborhoods due to redlining, we now have "risky" offers due to money. How much money someone has, where it comes from, and how easy it is to access is what we call modern-day redlining.

⸜⸝

"What if we find a way to change the DPA rules and restrictions to make it easier?" I asked my colleagues. That was answered with a quick no. The majority of DPAs are government funded, and changing them would be nearly impossible. But our group was not going to stop looking for ways to create change. It felt like we were trying to put a puzzle together, but we didn't have all the pieces.

Creative collaboration was the tool that made it all possible. There were two distinct barriers that we faced. First, we knew it needed to be a private fund so we could eliminate as many restrictions as possible. The fund needed to mirror family gifting without any requirement to pay it back.

Second, we needed to find an aligned partner so we could be unapologetic about serving families of color while complying with Fair Housing laws and offering the program to all families (no matter the race/ethnicity). We partnered with a local charter school, One City Schools, where 85% of the staff and families are Black and brown.

Once our focus became clear and we had the necessary people and funding to succeed, interest became evident, and we built out an education program for the families who were applying for the grant that included a racial-justice framework embedded in the financial literacy and homeownership learning.

⌇

But where would the money come from? This is when we saw that the community was ready for real change. At the very beginning we had gathered professionals together from different realty and financial institutions. It was the power of working within the industry, not within a specific company that was a game changer. As we talked to others in the real estate industry, in neighborhood and faith-based communities, we were shocked at how much money started coming in.

We had a seller donate $15,000 after he sold his family home and moved into a condo. A group of neighbors got together and donated $90,000! And a church shared the new program with their congregation and offered a $25,000 match. They ended up donating $70,000. By the time our first education program began, we had raised $350,000 in just six months. Today, we have real estate professionals contributing a percentage or a portion of all their closings to the fund, and consistent money is flowing in.

To date, ten families have become homeowners using the Own It down-payment grants, and hundreds of families are participating in the education offerings in hopes of one day applying for the program. These families have better opportunities to "own" real estate and create instant equity and the potential for generational wealth.

Below is the story of one of these homeowners, Jodie Pope, told in her own words. It provides the rest of the story.

❧

APPLYING THE ESSENTIAL ELEMENTS OF THE CHANGE FRAMEWORK

C (Community Change) = D (Desire) x V (Vision) x P (Power) (relationships plus action) > R Resistance

Actions are always political. By definition, being "political" (rooted in the Greek terms *polis* and *praxis)* means engaging in the practice of public life. It has little to do with what we call "partisan" or "electoral" politics. It is about using our power together to bring about positive change to our communities.

Therefore, the issues we decide to act upon together must be *actionable*:

1. Is the issue **clearly defined?** What is your aim?
2. Is the goal **significant?** Is it important enough for people to agree to act together to achieve?
3. Is the timeframe **immediate** enough?
4. Is the change we want **specific enough?** If not, can we break it down into several pieces?
5. Is the request or demand we are making **winnable with the power we have?** That is, can we actually do something about it?
6. Will success deepen and broaden the **engagement of our community?**

Politics:

The working together of citizens to get things done in their community.

---

cᕓᕤ

WHAT WE HAVE LEARNED

1. Actions must be aimed. Each action must have a **clear purpose and target.**

2. Actions are based on **knowing your assets/strengths** and building upon them. Each successful action should build support for you and your organization.

3. Activities are NOT actions if they do not bring us **significantly closer** to our vision. Going through the motions is simply not enough.

4. Every action should produce a reaction—either positive or negative. Learn to **anticipate it, welcome it, allow it to shape your next actions.**

5. Gauge your progress based on the **4 R's:**

6. How deep and broad is our network of **relationships** after the action?

7. Have you and your followers been **recognized**? Does the community know who you are and what you want?

8. Is there genuine **respect** between you and the people who are making the decisions?

9. Are you getting tangible **results** toward you goal or simple promises? How do you tell the difference?

10. Public action is the forge upon which trust and trustworthiness is measured and shaped. That is why **every action has to be followed by an evaluation** by you and your followers.

11. The learning that comes from acting and reflecting together becomes the building blocks for **developing future leaders** in your community.

cᕓᕤ

THE REST OF THE STORY
by Jodie Pope

My son Cameron and I were sitting in the parking lot of our condo. He read the sign at the edge of the parking lot and asked, "Mama, what does HOA stand for?" I responded, "Cam, it is an acronym for Home Owners Association." I went on to explain that everyone who lived in the rows of townhomes where we live were the owners of their houses and that we could all get together and, if most of us agreed, make rules about things like who mowed the lawns or if we could have dogs or cats in our houses.

As I had many times before, I shared with Cam that our goal was to live here for a few years and then buy another house and rent this one out to another family. I explained that we could then save some of the money we received in rent to buy another house and that one day this condo and anything else we accumulate would become his. I told him I wanted him to teach his children about how lots of people do this, just like I was doing with him right then.

It is said that owning a home is part of the American dream; a marker of success, an indicator that you have arrived. I also knew that it was one of the most important steps in creating what they call "generational wealth." I grew up in a home, and I am grateful for the stability that it provided, but my parents and I never had a conversation on homeownership or the benefits of it. I don't think they ever understood how to leverage homeownership to build up their equity. My siblings and I were not educated around the process, that's for sure.

At the time I had this conversation with Cam, I was a Black, 43-year-old, single woman, navigating this entire process blindly and by myself. It was all foreign to me, a process filled with anxiety and unknowns. I wanted to be intentional about involving my son in the process so that I could begin to normalize the home-buying process into something that people just did and everything it included.

☙

In 2019, as I was scrolling through Facebook, I glanced at a friend's post that intricately laid out her home-buying process including things about her realtor and mortgage lender. She described the emotionally-filled process, the barriers she faced, and how she had worked to overcome them. Her post stood out to me, and I knew that I wanted to buy someday but the thought was still just that.

Fast forward a few months, during the height of the COVID shutdown, it was a fall evening and I was again scrolling through Facebook (notice the pattern!). I came across an educational series that featured African Americans in the local real estate industry. This series introduced the concept of buying an owner-occupied multi-unit as an approach to investment opportunity. This approach to home ownership was something that I'd never thought about before and it became my primary interest as I continued to progress towards my own home ownership.

Without much knowledge on the homebuying front at the time, I kept the information that I was learning and the resources in a note-book. At some point, I pulled the notebook out and read the first step: Get your finances in order. I reached out to a local financial advisor and explained my goals. For the first time, I felt that I was heading in the right direction toward my future, and I started to investigate down-payment options. For weeks, I would search and email, only to be told that other than having 20% of the cost to put down, I was not eligible to buy a house.

⌒⌇⌒

From society's viewpoint, I felt I'd done everything right. I had a full-time job, a pension, health, renters, and life insurance. I was college educated, earning a decent income, and had proven myself to be responsible and accountable. But still, I could not manage to save much for a down-payment on my first home. With my income, I was not eligible for any financial down-payment assistance programs. Despite saving a portion of my paycheck every month, and all the stimulus payments for my son and I during COVID, it seemed that it would still take years to save enough cash to make the sizeable down-payment that seemed to be required of every first-time home buyer.

Enter the organization Own-It: Building Black Wealth. In the fall of 2021, I received an email from my son's school about a new pro-gram whose mission is to increase Black homeownership in Dane County, Wisconsin. The program offered an eight-week financial planning series lead by a financial planner and then, for participants who were ready for the next phase, a four-week home buying course led by local real estate professionals. With successful completion of both training sessions and a mortgage pre-approval letter, you could then apply for a $15,000 grant with no additional eligibility require-ments. As I sat in the long line of cars for pick-up at Cam's school,

I read this email and cried. This could be the final piece I needed to buy a home! The program was intentional; it provided support, insider knowledge, resources, and—of course—that critical $15,000 I didn't have.

As I went through the Own-It process, I became more confident. Learning the "insider" vocabulary gave me a sense of what to expect. I also received connections to people who would and could support me in buying a home.

I put in an offer in October 2022 and closed on our first home a few weeks later. Already, I have successfully changed a showerhead, replaced a screen on my screen door, painted, hung drywall, refinished a patio table. And I learn more about being a homeowner every day.

Most importantly, I learned that change can happen—if we each take action, one step at a time.

꒰ꔛ꒱

ACTIVATION

Below find some "think" and "do" activities to help you **deal with your own understanding and feelings** about action as opposed to activity.

THINK

1. What actions you have already taken? What was the reaction to each, good or bad? How can you **better design future actions** with what you have learned?
2. From a leadership perspective, who have you already recruited and who might you be ready to invite? Do you need any encouragement or training? **Who might provide it?**
3. Plan your next action by remembering these core questions: What action can you do with what you already have? What help do you need to have an **even more successful action?** Where can you get that help?

DO

1. Have a mini-retreat with your core group to **assess how things are going** with your campaign. Review actions taken, relationships built, and current status of your community change.

2. Decide your next shared action plan. How will you recruit people, what will you ask for, who will lead the event, what will they say, how will you end? **Role play the event.**

3. Set a time to review **the action and the reaction;** learn from what happened, decide your next steps.

RESISTANCE

CHAPTER 7

"R" IS FOR RESISTANCE

Resistance: the opposition that occurs when
there is a shift in the status quo

People don't resist change.
They resist being changed.

Peter Senge, *The Fifth Discipline*

Sometimes we are seeking change because of a deeply felt dream or desire or discontent.

But we find that others resist the change we are proposing by expressing their dissatisfaction with the disruption of the status quo. This is a universal, complicated, natural, and an inevitable reaction to a feeling of losing control. We even have an acronym for this: NIMBY (Not In My Back Yard).

So if we are trying to make community change it is better to anticipate resistance than to be blindsided by it. One of the fundamental maxims of systems change is that the harder you push the system, the harder the system pushes back. So how do we lean into resistance— not fear it, but embrace it as inevitable and natural?

SUCH IS THE SKULL OF A FINLANDER
by Will Andresen

I had just sat down on day one of my new job as the Chamber of Commerce director in Ironwood, an old mining town in Michigan's Upper Peninsula, a place three generations deep into a bust cycle.

I knew no one, and didn't know where to start. And then in walks Larry Peterson.

In that two-hour visit, Larry shared with me his dream of honoring the community's heritage in order to reverse the town's decline. The next day, he came back to apologize for taking so much of my time, and then he spent three more hours describing his dream! At a time when historic buildings were being demolished left and right, it was a hard dream to envision. But Larry's passion was crystal clear.

⌁

Larry never left town after the mines closed, unlike so many others who did. He's not a government official. Not a business owner. Doesn't have a degree in community development. Not a community organizer or a politician. But the man has his own set of gifts that he offers to the community. To begin with, he has a vision, and the passion to pursue his vision. His eyes light up when he tells stories of the Al Capone days or when Abbott and Costello performed at the packed Historic Ironwood Theatre. "We need to reveal and not conceal our history, Will," he tells me. "We need to collect, salvage and use whatever we can. That's our path to the future."

Resistance to change is strong everywhere. People naturally fight it for a slew of conscious and unconscious reasons, some real and some imaginary. But Larry will tell you it's especially strong in his home town: "The mining companies provided everything, your house your school, everything. They even determined the color of your toilet seat: Managers got white seats; miners got red. In return, they took your soul. Right from the start, we were owned by someone else."

Larry says this led to a culture of "passive resistance." His solution was gathering what he called "like-minded doers" to work together. But even their collaborative efforts were stymied by one of the community's mining legacies—the intentional ethnic clustering of people to keep them separated and keep them from organizing.

⁓

Despite these passive and active forces of resistance, Larry Peterson persevered. A gifted raconteur, Larry tells the story of a Finnish miner who fell down a mine shaft, propelling head-first through scaffolding and crashing to the bottom of the pit. The men who scrambled down a ladder to retrieve his remains discovered the miner already climbing back up, with only minor abrasions to his tongue. The next day, a newspaper headline declared "Such is the skull of a Finlander."

In his own community change efforts, Larry felt like that Finn "pretty much all the time." When asked why he kept climbing back out of the pit, Larry would say he was doing it for his grandchildren. But upon deeper investigation, I learned that it's just who Larry is. "I'm a rebel, a perpetual gadfly," he told me. "I enjoy mixing it up. I like the struggles, like the challenges. I don't give up and I can't sit still."

Larry didn't give up, patiently sharing his gifts to nudge positive change wherever he could. For thirty-two years he's been doing a twice-weekly radio show "to create unity in the community." His show was designed not just to inform his neighbors but to inspire them. To make them feel proud of their history so they could build upon it. He would tell stories of how two railroad lines had to be built in order to haul so much ore out of town. How we might have lost both world wars if it wasn't for our area's iron ore being used to build ships and tanks and planes. How Ironwood's citizens built a Memorial Building honoring fallen World War I soldiers that far outsized Chicago's.

But that's not all. For nine years, Larry taught local history at the community college, climbing through attics and basements to find material to build his curriculum. Always, he said, encouraging his students to look at the past with an eye to the future. Whenever asked, he would lead highly popular walking tours of the sites of local speak-easies, complete with stories about dead gangsters and show-girls to build wonder in our past. Also a talented artist, he donated drawings to help fund renovations to local historic buildings like the Ironwood Memorial Building, the Ironwood Carnegie Library, and the Ironwood Depot Museum.

More than once I was on the receiving end of Larry's firmly shared conviction that I could do more and better in my official capacities!

⌇⌇

Larry taught, inspired, gave, and extolled. But he acknowledged that others needed to do the same. Enter Ivan Hellen and Rick Semo and the story of the Miners Memorial Heritage Park.

When the mines finally closed in the 1960s, they left behind a 300-acre parcel of subsided land and mining rubble in the heart of the city. For decades, the "caves" were used as a landfill, compost site, and illegal dumping ground for both snow and junk. Forty years later, however, a new idea surfaced, an idea built on the opportunities that had been left behind. By then, all the mines on the site had been completely abandoned and were filled with water. This created beautiful ponds framed by majestic rock outcroppings. Reclaiming their rightful place, vegetation covered much of the vacant land.

The new idea, fostered by Ivan and Rick, asked why we couldn't build trails and do so in a way that honored the 1100 miners who had died below ground? This wasn't just going to be another park with another trail. It was going to be hallowed ground, where people of today could connect with people of yesterday. Said Ivan: "Finding and exposing these mining sites was critical to bringing our history back. Building rubble into a monument just strikes the imagination."

But their idea was met with significant resistance. Both passive and active resistance, as Larry had warned. And that is the rest of the story.

꒳

APPLYING THE ESSENTIAL ELEMENTS OF THE CHANGE FRAMEWORK

C (Community Change) = D (Desire) x V (Vision) x P (Power) (relationships plus action) > R Resistance

One of the brutal lessons of leading change is that being right, being just, and being polite doesn't guarantee success. Like in baseball you can have everything right—focus, equipment, strategy, physical attributes, mental attitude, etc.—and still strike out or pop up or a hundred other scenarios about 2/3 of the time.

Many of us struggle with this reality, particularly when a cause we think is motherhood and apple pie is resisted, dismissed or rejected. How dare they! Don't they get it? Why can't they see what we see? Whether it's housing the homeless, starting an after-school program, assuring clean drinking water for our kids, being able to walk safely in our neighborhood, or taking on the bullies at school or a thousand other worthy causes—nothing replaces that shock of being told NO.

It is the death of innocence and the realization that, in the world as it is, power is the currency of the realm, not righteousness, niceness, or justice. These teachable moments—where you operate in the gap between the world as we would like it to be and the world as it is—are rich in learning. But only if we are willing to embrace tension as a healthy condition of any change worthy of our efforts.

It is in these moments that the real test of leadership happens. As the old Kenny Rogers' song goes, "You got to know when to hold 'em, know when to fold 'em, know when to walk away, and know when to run." Do we fold, walk or run away? Sometimes. But if we want to change things, we have to overcome resistance.

People who work for community change knows that the powers-that-be concede nothing without a fight. There are no free lunches or immaculate conceptions, only the opportunity for us to pursue justice…if we are willing to rekindle our passion, be persistent, and patiently pursue the change we are seeking.

We have seen the power of these moments. They define our character and serve as the forge upon which resilient leadership is tempered over time through successes and yes, occasional failures. This is politics (community involvement) in its original form: unvarnished, raucous, and raw. It tests the sunshine soldier, the weekend warrior, and the hobbyists who are good at the book club banter but in the heat of battle seek cover.

So, embrace the NO, knowing that the YES will be that much sweeter because you earned it. And in the process, you will build a stronger community.

༒

WHAT WE HAVE LEARNED

1. Every action has a reaction. When you take action to clean up the creek, champion fixing up your neighborhood park, or confront the bully at school, no matter how just you may think your cause may be, be prepared for resisters to question your actions. Anticipate it, understand it, and **prepare actions you might take to embrace a healthy tension.**

2. Don't take it personally. Stay focused on your vision. Remember that people are busy; **you must inspire them with a dream that is worthy of their efforts.** How can their individual concerns be incorporated into the shared vision?

3. Engage the resistors early and often. **Be proactive. Listen, learn, understand, and make adjustments.** You may find that others want to have a voice in shaping the vision and the subsequent action.

4. Work to find common ground before rushing to judgment. **Maybe there are ideas embedded in the opposition that could make your vision even better.**

5. If you can pilot-test the change on a small scale, **demonstrate the benefits/advantages, using language familiar to all the stakeholders,** to create a visual or simple narrative explaining the positive impact of the change you are proposing.

6. Remember: the bigger the change, the stronger the resistance. If you can, take it one bite at a time while building trust as you engage in action. **All change happens at the speed of relationships.** Remember the universals of relationships: All relationships are built on trust and forged in action. Your first action priority, therefore, always should be building relationships.

Resistance is the opposition that occurs when there is a shift in the status quo

---

THE REST OF THE STORY

Ivan and Rick—like Larry—were sons of miners who grew up in the area. Initially Rick Semo was most excited about trails in the park, but he grew more and more intrigued by the historical aspect of the effort. "I grew up here, but wasn't aware of what makes us 'us'; why Ironwood is different from other places."

Ivan Hellen was at the very forefront of the idea, attending the first meeting of just a few like-minded people. Including Rick. One of their first steps was to hold a ski/hike/snowshoe at the proposed park so "people could see the possibilities" and "to get more people involved." Building on the success of this first effort, the two guys hosted a screening of the new film "A Town Called Ironwood" at the Historic Ironwood Theatre that successfully recruited even more like-minded people. Quickly, the group organized itself into a non-profit entity called the "Friends of the Miners Memorial Heritage Park."

The Friends group went to the local governing body, asking them to officially set aside the land as a heritage park. They had filled the room with supporters, yet the city commissioners voted it down. I attended this meeting and walked away disappointed. Rick also attended; but he didn't walk away. Instead he was inspired to move from being a citizen to becoming a politician and running for a seat on the very commission that had turned down the park proposal.

Along with several others similarly called to action, the makeup of the commission was changed virtually overnight. And Heritage Park was approved by a unanimous vote.

ᴄᴊ⁾⁾ᴅ

As a newly elected city commissioner, Rick Semo was eager to make more people aware of the park's potential. So he got himself out there on the site, envisioning where to build the trails. He moved a few logs, threw some across a small stream to build a makeshift bridge, and woke up the next morning to see a front-page, above the fold, World War II-sized headline proclaiming him a "trail blazer." But, complete with a photo of his log "bridge," it wasn't a positive story. Rick had been hoping to encourage slow, steady progress on the park, but this headline "blew everything up." Resistance intensified.

Much had to happen to fight this reaction. Early on, to address the passive resistance of apathy, the Friends group worked to build public understanding, enthusiasm and support by holding weekly walking tours, sponsoring scholarships for mining descendants, manning informational booths at local festivals and fairs, entering floats in local parades and sponsoring work bees and clean-up days.

The active resistance to the proposed heritage park focused on issues such as safety, user-conflicts, and government finances. The group addressed these concerns in a number of ways. When local officials were concerned about safety, Ivan walked the area with them, showing where the mine entrances were (and weren't) to help allay their fears. Rick and other early-supporters traveled to another Upper Peninsula community that had already built a similar park and trail project and came back with viable solutions to address the safety concerns. When motorized users pushed back at the planned non-motorized trails, Rick met with them, patiently listened, built relationships, and eventually agreed on a compromise. To address charges regarding the waste of public dollars, the Friends group agreed to raise the funds to both build and maintain the heritage park.

Today, the Miners Memorial Heritage Park in Ironwood, Michigan, is being enjoyed for all of its intended purposes. And much more. A regional cross-country ski race runs right through the park. Youth trail-running and mountain-biking clubs practice weekly. An annual arts festival hosts a popular Art in the Park exhibit and Kids' Story Walk. And a butterfly garden now welcomes all visitors.

Rick told me that the best way to fight resistance is to show results. "You're not going to convince most people with just the idea or good arguments," he says. "Other people may just not see it. You need to fight the good fight. Be positive, improve bit by bit." Both Ivan and Rick agreed that the effort's ultimate success resulted from the community's increased sense of ownership as it struggled to address the not inconsiderable resistance. As time went on, trail advocates, history buffs, and nature-lovers have all coalesced into a strong band of supporters that insures the park's future.

⌇⌇⌇

Larry Peterson used the gifts he was given to lonely-push against the granite. When the granite showed signs of bending, others leaned in too. The granite fully bent when the very culture of the community evolved to embracing a strong future built around its proud past and inherent strengths. According to Rick, "Larry inspired all of us to action. And he helped us to understand our history and culture throughout this project. Our community pride has definitely grown."

Much has happened in Larry's hometown since he first walked into my office thirty years ago. Renovations have been made to the Historic Ironwood Theatre to keep the place hopping. A strong majority of voters voted to place an additional tax on themselves to restore the magnificent Ironwood Memorial Building. Mining murals and historic signage have gone up. Refurbished and brand-new museums are now telling new stories of the old days. Paved walking trails now travel along an abandoned rail line and restored trestles connect the Miners Park to historic downtowns and neighborhoods.

Pulling together has brought new life back to Ironwood. New businesses are sprouting up in the historic downtown. Old houses are being restored to welcome new residents. The city's century-long population decline is finally projected to reverse. Larry Peterson always claimed he was not a sage sitting on a mountain—just a person who works hard. He still shares his dreams and his passions and his gifts everywhere he can. And he perseveres. Such is the skull of Larry Peterson.

ACTIVATION

Below find some "think" and "do" activities to help you **deal with your own understanding and feelings** about resistance you might encounter in trying to bring about community change.

THINK

1. What experiences **in either your public or your private life** can you draw upon where you addressed someone else's resistance or doubt to something? What did you do? What did you learn?
2. What resistance can you **anticipate or even imagine** to your proposed change or changes?
3. What relationships do you have that might help you address the resistance? (If you don't have any, **go get some before proceeding with your action.**)

DO

1. Bring your core leaders together and **refresh your relational map** to pinpoint potential resistance as you work on your action campaign.
2. As you start to act, assess where any resistance is coming from. Is it from where you expected it? **Is it overt or covert?**
3. What actions can you take to reduce resistance or find ways of seeking common ground? **Ask yourself if you are willing to compromise,** even on things you really want but could live without.
4. After you have accomplished your dream or addressed your discontent on something in your community, **how do you reestablish relationships** important to your community with those who opposed you?

CONCLUSION

꩜

BRINGING IT ALL TOGETHER

by Tom Mosgaller and Mike Breininger

End—the time right before beginning again

Do not go gentle into that good night.
Rage, rage against the dying of the light.

Dylan Thomas

"So, how's it going?" That is the question we are often asked when we are in the midst of something we are doing in and for our community. We hope this Handbook has given you a fresh set of eyes for answering this question.

As Abraham Lincoln observed, there will always be swamps, deserts, and chasms to deal with; but there will also be dreams, dry land, and bridges that will make it well worth your while to step up, step in, and step out to make a difference in your community.

The question should shift to "How you will be able to maintain your momentum." It would be disheartening to think you came this far, learned so much, built all these relationships, created your own story, and then just went gentle into the night.

෮ℐℴ

There are seven lessons we would like to leave you with as you continue your community change work.

1. Use the Change Framework to assess, refresh, and refine your organizing: **Community Change = D x V x P (r+a) > R.**
2. **Relationship-building is your superpower.** Never stop doing-one-to-one relational meetings. Do them before you need them, not after.
3. Action is to your community-change work **as oxygen is to your human body.**
4. Have a plan, act on it, learn from the reactions, and improve. **Make continuous improvement part of your DNA.**
5. Continuous learning is **the lifeblood of healthy leaders** and **the secret sauce of strong communities.** Build learning opportunities into everything you do.
6. Flip on your dream switch. **Be bold, try new things, follow your passions.**
7. Start with what you've got, before talking about what you need. **Every community already has more assets and gifts than it imagines.**

෮ℐℴ

Contributors to this book include:

Sara Alvarado is a writer, speaker, entrepreneur, and fierce advocate for racial justice in real estate. She believes that the way to handle challenges in life and business is to show up authentic, bold, vulnerable, and always ready for fun.

For over thirty-five years, **Will Andresen** has collaborated with local communities and non-profit organizations in creating high impact, outcome-driven community development initiatives. His career focused on asset-based community development in rural and remote communities. After retiring as Director of the University of Wisconsin's Institute of Community Development, he continues to advocate for positive asset-based change in his Upper Peninsula community.

Mike Breininger and his wife, Christy, have raised sixteen children and cared for and/or mentored over 100 foster children, international exchange students, and young adults. Mike is the pastor of a nondenominational church, New House Richland, in Richland Center, Wisconsin. He has nearly four decades of being the administrator of a private school, Eagle School International, and is founder and president of Southwest Partners, a regional community development organization. Mike is a founding member of Wisconsin Partners, a statewide partnership of associations, and the founder and leader of the Midwest Regional Hub, which cooperatively brings together church and marketplace leaders. He has worked as the board chair for economic development for the City of Richland Center and for Richland County. Mike is an international teacher and trainer for Youth With A Mission and other organizations.

Michele Engh is an ELCA Pastor living in the Driftless Region of Southwest Wisconsin with her **husband Pete.** She is a mother of five and has a career path that includes nursing, youth ministry, and community development. Michelle is passionate about building relationships across silos and other barriers because it is only in relationships that we can bring about positive change.

Tommy Enright is a farmer, advocate, and Communications Director for Wisconsin Farmers Union. He lives on a small farm in Central Wisconsin with his spouse, **Sam,** and their two sons.

Kristen Joiner has co-founded multiple environmental and social impact ventures, a non-profit organization, and a school. Scenarios USA, the non-profit she started with **producer Maura Minsky,** is recognized for pioneering a human-rights approach to comprehensive sexuality education, currently being scaled to global implementation by the WHO and UNFPA. Under her leadership, the private/public partnership for climate change developed by the Wisconsin environmental organization, Sustain Dane, was selected as a national model by the Obama Administration. Kristen wrote former Obama Administration Representative for International Disability Rights, **Judy Heumann's,** two memoirs: *Being Heumann* (Beacon Press) and *Rolling Warrior* (YA -Beacon Press). *Being Heumann* was optioned by Apple TV and is currently in pre-development by the Oscar-winning filmmaker, **Sian Heder.** Kristan lives in Auckland, New Zealand, with her family and a pup who looks like a sheep.

John McKnight is co-founder of the Asset Based Community Development Institute (ABCD) and is recognized globally as a community development visionary, sage, and storyteller. John co-authored the original basic ABCD guide *Building Communities from the Inside Out* and its current version *The Connected Community.*

Tom Mosgaller is an experienced community builder, teacher, and leader who believes that the power of relationships is the cornerstone of strong, vibrant communities. Tom has led, taught, and coached community builders in the art of pulling together in places both big and small, urban and rural, locally, and internationally. He has celebrated successes and learned from setbacks that inspired the timeless lessons captured in the Change Framework that serves as the backbone of *Pulling Together*. He is past president of the American Society for Quality (ASQ), and co-author of the recently published book on institutional change: *Bending Granite*. Tom has led and served on numerous educational, healthcare, governmental, faith-based, and agricultural boards. When Tom is not leading, teaching, and working with others, he can be found learning from the land and animals on his farm in the Driftless Area of Wisconsin.

Jodie Pope is a higher education professional and a proud mother to her son, Cameron. She enjoys traveling, laughing, listening to music, and embracing her creative side.

Paul Terranova is the Midwest Community Organizer for Manufactured Housing Action (MHAction). Prior to that, he spent twenty years bringing an organizing lens to community center work at the Lussier Community Education Center in Madison, WI. Earlier in his career, he worked as a youth organizer with El Centro Hispano (Durham, North Carolina), a refugee job developer with Lutheran Family Services, a tenant organizer with the North Carolina Low Income Housing Coalition, a public action organizer with the United Farmworkers of America AFL-CIO, and a volunteer support worker with children living on the streets in Cape Town, South Africa. Paul lives in Madison with his **wife Nancy.**

Jeff Yost is President and CEO of the Nebraska Community Foundation (NCF). For the past 25 years NCF has inspired leaders and residents in over 250 Nebraska communities to take charge, inspire change, and stimulate their local economies.

Thank you for the opportunity to share this Handbook with you. As generations of community changers who came before us have taught: Leave things better than you found them, and don't forget to pass this idea on to the next generation. If you have any questions, reactions, or stories to share about leading community change, send an email to **pulling-together@actapublications.com** or visit our website at **www.pulling-together.com**. We promise we'll answer you!